Teaching for Learning

Louis E. Raths
State University College
Fredonia, New York

Charles E. Merrill Publishing Company
A Bell & Howell Company
Columbus, Ohio

The Coordinated Teacher Preparation Series
Under the Editorship of
Donald E. Orlosky
University of South Florida
and
Ned B. MacPhail
Depauw University

Copyright © 1969 by Louis E. Raths. All rights reserved. No part of this book may be reproduced in any form, electronic or mechanical, including protocopy, recording, or any information storage and retrieval system, without permission in writing from the publisher.

Standard Book Number: 675-09417-8

Library of Congress Card Number: 79-95170

1 2 3 4 5 6 7 8 9 10 / 73 72 71 70 69

Printed in the United States of America

To *Professor Frederick E. Hahn*
of Upsala College

who has shown a deep and continuing concern that these ideas should be shared with a wider public and with institutions which have the responsibility for preparing teachers.

Acknowledgments

My deepest obligations are to the many hundreds of teachers who have participated in the formulation of this functional analysis of *teaching*. I am also very grateful to the graduate students in education at the Ohio State University and at New York University who, over a period of many years, gave much time and effort to the critical analysis of these materials.

I acknowledge with sincere thanks the cooperation given me by the schools of Roselle Park, N. J., under the administration of Mr. John S. Linscott, Jr., and the staff of The Intermediate School of East Orange, N. J., whose principal is Mr. Noble R. Young and whose assistant principal is Mr. Samuel L. Bishop. These schools participated in a final trial of the ideas presented in this book.

Professor Arnold Rothstein of City College, New York City, and Professor Selma Wasserman of Simon Fraser University, British Columbia, read and commented on the manuscript. I deeply appreciate their interest and concern.

Mrs. Ruth Harte assumed complete responsibility for preparing a preliminary edition of the present volume. I am very grateful to her for her patience and hard work.

Preface

For a long time, with regard to our approaches to teaching, we teachers have had the cart before the horse. We have talked about *good* teaching before we have made it clear just what we mean by *teaching*. Is it possible to get substantial agreement on what teaching should be?

The age in which we now live has been characterized in many ways. It has been called the Age of Technology, the Age of Affluence, and so forth. It might also be called the Age of Widespread Education. There is little doubt that technology has contributed most to the phenomenon called the "knowledge explosion" and the to affluence of the Western World. There is at the same time an awareness that poverty and ignorance go together. If poverty is to be substantially reduced, those in the poverty categories must participate in a higher quality and quantity of education.

Our age has also been called the Age of Bureaucracy. The dehumanization resulting from bureaucracy has brought about a great deal of dissent which reveals itself in the marked resistance to university authorities and governmental actions. Moreover this resistance to arbitrary decisions from the top down seems to be a worldwide phenomenon. Our age has also been referred to as the Age of Anxiety, or the Sick Society. The pressures to succeed in a competitive world take their toll; nowadays many more people suffer from emotional and 'mental' disturbances. The behavior of school age children reflects this problem; they have more emotional problems than did previous generations.

What kind of education and what kind of teaching will best aid us in ushering in a better world? Education is a composite of content and the ways by which we acquire it—a combining of means and ends. At its best it is a series of worthwhile experiences which enables students to grow and mature. But instead of trying to define education in the abstract, it is suggested that every school inquire into its own content and methods. If the principal and the faculty of a school keep appropriate records, they will soon find out what sort of education is going on in that school.

In this volume the emphasis has been placed upon teaching which will help to meet the needs of the individual in our ever changing, dehumanized society. Accordingly, a set of teaching functions is presented which considers the student's emotional needs, the use of thinking processes, the diagnosis of learning difficulties, the clarification of human values, development of group power and morale, status within the group, and the relations between school and community. All in all, ten components of teaching are discussed; in each case, these components can easily be identified by an observer in the classroom. In addition, a word to boards of education, superintendents, and principals on the importance of reporting and recording has been included in the last chapter.

At present, we need facts about teaching. We need to ask the pertinent questions and collect the relevant evidence about what teaching is and what it should be. It is my hope that this little book will help and stimulate a widespread inquiry into the processes of *teaching*.

Louis E. Raths
July, 1969

Contents

1	The Changing Character of Education	1
2	Awakening Concerns About Teaching	15
3	The Ten Components of Teaching	23
4	Components 1-4: Classroom Procedures	33
5	Components 5-6: Relating to the Outside World	45
6	Components 7-8: Security Among One's Peers	61
7	Components 9-10: Helping Students to Learn and Grow	77
8	For Boards of Education, Superintendents, and Principals	95
	References	102
	Index	103

1

The Changing Character of Education

PRESSURES UPON THE SCHOOLS

The American financial investment in education is huge, and year by year it is growing larger. The fact that education is necessary to virtually every aspect of modern life helps to accounts for this growth. Education is needed to obtain employment and to enter institutions of higher learning. The advancement of knowledge and its practical applications and the wise use of natural and human resources depend directly upon education. In short, education is necessary simply to understand the increasingly complex world in which we live. All of these factors have combined to put pressure upon schools, teachers, and administrators to adapt their educational programs to our ever changing, constantly expanding world.

There are other pressures, too. This is a time of intense international conflict that is widely publicized by practically all media of communication. Do the Russians educate more effectively than we do? Are the Chinese catching up with us, and will they soon excel? Isn't education the first line of defense? To be strong, must we not offer the very best training to scientists, mathematicians, and engineers?

During this century alone the increase in knowledge has been tremendous. No one today can claim *all knowledge* as his field. In fact, practically no one can claim *all mathematics*, or *all physics*, or *all literature* as his field. The mere organizing and storing of all this information has become a very complex problem. There is a continuing revision of past interpretations of history; "new" history is being created day by day. Great additions are being made to our stores of fiction, drama, and poetry. There is much that is new in the fields of art, music, dance, and architecture. Mathematics and the sciences have become vast fields of knowledge and exploration. The point is very clear: we can no longer say that we are passing on to a new generation all that is known about any of these fields. The "knowledge explosion" continues to explode, and because of it we will have to reexamine the aims of teaching. It is impossible to teach all of it. What shall we choose to teach, and how will we decide?

If we look around us, we will see and feel more pressure upon each of us to think about what we should do in our schools. We are informed by seemingly reliable sources that there has been a great increase in crime and that much of this crime is being committed by young people. We are all familiar with the increased emphasis upon violence. The problem of racism in our country has reached alarming proportions. A national determination to extend democracy abroad through resort to wars of various kinds is proving to be self-defeating, and human life itself becomes less precious in the process.

There has been a great decline in the influence of the church. Within the past several generations the family has undergone significant change: many more mothers are employed, and the fathers tend to commute to their work and hence see less of their children than formerly. Mental illness has increased very much and has contributed to the instability of family life. Divorce is more frequent. One could go on and on, cataloguing symptoms of our "sick" society, all of them suggesting that perhaps the schools should teach something about the pathology of our culture. But what shall we choose to emphasize, and how shall we make the decision?

The Influence of the Communication Media

In terms of its direct impact upon the lives of children, perhaps the most significant of all changes is associated with the media of communication. Children now listen to the radio and watch television more hours each week than they spend in school. On the TV screen children see people with whom they identify, killing, lying, cheating, stealing, double-crossing each other—acting in ways which we generally associate with a sick society. Are television and radio reflecting this kind of a society? Are they contributing to its development?

We all know that the primary aim of these media is to sell merchandise for the business interests of the world, and thus to make money—for the station, the network, the manufacturers, the distributors, the advertising community, and the stockholders. To attract listening and viewing audiences in larger and larger numbers, the programmers pander to the lowest of tastes. More and more violence is shown, and this violence characterizes the behavior of "good guys" as well as "bad guys." In other words, decision makers feel that there is nothing wrong with violence—it brings in an audience, doesn't it? And (most importantly) it increases sales and profits.

And yet the waywardness continues. Children see how trucks are hi-jacked, how banks are robbed, how burglaries are planned and carried through, how riots are fostered and continued. They see defiance of law and authority in ever so many areas of life. They see unfaithful wives and husbands. They see what is for them a most unusual emphasis upon sex, and they see the reactions of adults to these sexual stimuli.

As they listen and watch, children are actually in association with depraved creatures of many kinds. They are in the presence of people without values. They see authority flouted, often with impunity. What is significant about all this? *For the first time in the history of the world* children are having valuelessness placed directly before them. They are seeing and hearing and feeling about this world they never made. So drastic a change in the lives of children makes it necessary for us to modify our school programs and reexamine our ideas about teaching.

Radio and television are influential educators, and compete intensely with the schools in promoting a way of life. That these media are successful in selling goods and making money, no one will deny. That they are also successful (without aiming to be) in influencing the lives of children, their growth, and development goes without saying. Of course there are good programs for both children and adults on radio and television. But these represent a small proportion of the total fare, and children are indiscriminate watchers—they see and hear just about everything that is offered. What can the schools do in the face of such powerful competition?

The Changing School Community

Our world is very different from what it was fifty years ago. The schools have changed in many ways. Since they are much larger than they used to be, they put new demands upon children. There are many more special services in the schools, and this probably influences our concept of teaching. The growth of the cities and the suburbs has resulted in significant changes in the recruiting of teachers. There was a time when a great many teachers were born and brought up in the communities in which they teach, but now this is less likely to be true. Today teachers drive to their schools and drive home again at the end of the day. Very often, they drive somewhere away from the school for lunch. They are not closely identified with the community and are more distant from the lives of the children whom they teach.

In spite of all the *social* and *technological* change that has taken place, there has been very little change in the teaching that goes on in our schools. There have been great changes in the training of social workers, nurses, physicians, and engineers and scientists, generally speaking. But there have been very few significant changes in the education of teachers. The new conditions of life for all people in general, and for children and teachers in particular, suggest very clearly the necessity for positive changes in school programs and in our concepts of teaching. While the pressures around us have increased our tensions and anxieties, they have not resulted in wholesome changes in our ways of working with a new generation of children and a new generation of parents. What is teaching today? What should it be?

THE UNIVERSITIES AND TEACHING

One slogan has it that wars are too important to be left to the decisions of generals. Are educational problems too important to be left to the decisions of educators? Ideally, shouldn't these problems be referred to a community of scholars—a place where philosophers, scientists, historians, anthropologists, mathematicians, sociologists, linguists, specialists in language and literature, law, medicine, and religion are all in association with each other? In other words, isn't it reasonable to look to the universities for guidance and help?

Oddly enough, as a group, they seem to be as confused as any of us. In the present decade there have been ever so many student protests and a number of student rebellions in several countries of the world, including our own. Students are protesting about the kind of education they are getting; they want to participate in making policy decisions about educational offerings and about their lives as members of that community of scholars.

The Changing Character of Education

It is fairly well known that faculties in the institutions are also going through a period of great unrest. They too want to have a greater share in the management of the institutions of higher learning. They feel that important educational decisions are now made by administrators who have little or no contact with students, who do not themselves teach, and who are out of contact with the disciplines represented in the university. They see their institutions being managed as a "business," and they believe this to be wrong in principle and stultifying in practice.

In their very earliest days universities had vocational objectives, but these were very limited in number: the university prepared students in the areas of law, religion, medicine, and teaching. They also had a curriculum known as the liberal arts. Today the university prepares for a great many professions and vocations and the curriculum is determined largely by *departmental* interests. Today's complex university has lost sight of the concern of the students and a few faculty members for a "liberal education" due to the pressures of vocationalism and the vested interests of the departmental organization.

The graduate school is commonly regarded as the villain in the present situation. It has been most responsive to governmental pressures for new instruments and techniques for making war. For many years the national government has subsidized its activities heavily. *Research* is not only emphasized; it has become the conveyor belt of financial support from the national government. In some of our most prestigious universities the research budgets have represented a tremendous outlay of money, time, and effort, and the costs are almost entirely met by the national government.

To be a "successful" professor, one had to participate in many of these new ventures. One had to prepare projects and submit them for approval to representatives of scientific groups, who in turn would submit them to governmental decision makers. "Successful" professors brought money and prestige to the campus. They also brought many new people to the campus, and *on paper* these new additions became members of the faculty. Many of them, however, did little teaching, if any, and were not integrated into the community of scholars. The faculty, as a group, began to lose its identity and its dedication to the college community. Its primary sources of support were elsewhere, presumably.

Great emphasis was placed upon whether or not a faculty member had "published." An old saying was revived, polished up, and badly misinterpreted: *Publish or perish.* In its original meaning it had emphasized the idea that writing out one's ideas and submitting them to the critical scrutiny of one's peers is not only a form of self-discipline but also the single best way of remaining alive intellectually. If one publishes, one is involved with a community of scholars, one is *alive*. Without publishing, a professor is apt to stagnate, to slip into practices where he is no longer under the critical scrutiny of his colleagues.

Today that old slogan is interpreted differently. Now it is taken to mean that if you want a good professorial position, your chances are enhanced if you have published a number of articles, a book or two, or a series of research reports. It is taken to mean that promotion within the college or university depends upon whether or not one has indeed published. And it is the *number* of publications which has grown in importance—not the quality of them. Little or no inquiry is made of what one's peers actually think of the writings.

In the two developments just discussed—subsidized research and publications—there is an underlying ramification of great import. The college and the university are beginning to abdicate their own responsibilities in judging the worth of their faculties. They are surrendering significant power to sources *outside* their jurisdiction. Were those who benefited from project support and those who published making significant contributions to the education of students? Were they enhancing the quality of living on the college campus? Were they recognizing the prime importance of teaching? Were they keeping in touch with student life and culture? Were they aware of the changing needs of the new generation of students? In most cases the answer is an emphatic *no*. Nevertheless, outside financial support and a list of publications have become more and more important in deciding who will be promoted, and in many cases, who will be appointed to positions on the faculty.

As was mentioned before, a third indication of the befuddlement of our community of scholars is to be found in their development and acceptance of what constitutes a *college education*. In this respect one must take into consideration the central role of departments in the organization of colleges and universities. Departments are *the* core of the university establishment. They are the real decision makers when it comes to matters of curriculum and teaching; they are the prime movers in setting up qualifications for teaching and for promotions. They alone decide on the requirements for degrees, for majors and minors, for passing and failing, and for many other relevant decision areas.

As the numbers of students who attend college has increased, so also have the numbers within departments increased. As more and more time has been devoted to the discovery of new facts and information, there has been a trend toward the proliferation of new courses within each department. After students have taken the required one or two basic courses, they are often allowed to choose from a tremendous variety of courses offered by the department.

It has been taken for granted that subject matter as such is educational, that it can be divided up into quantitative units, and that a certain number of units from one department, when added to the units accumulated in other departments, constitutes a college education—*higher* education, in fact. A student who has amassed a certain number of points and who has managed to keep up his membership in the community is thus certified for a degree.

A President of the United States once remarked that the best kind of education would have Mark Hopkins at one end of a log and a student at the other. He did *not* say what Mark Hopkins was doing at his end. We should forgive him for the omission, and we should thank him for the respect he showed teaching. We might also wish that educational administrators everywhere were equally devoted to the important role of teaching in the organized processes of education.

The University Bureaucracy

The colleges and universities, these communities of scholars, have revealed their confusion and administrative irresponsibility toward education in a number of ways. Colleges once guarded entrance to the sacred portals by requiring a certain number of Carnegie units in a variety of subject matter fields. Later, they chose college entrance exams, composed and administered by a central but outside committee. These tests tended to emphasize information, not knowledge and skills. Such quantitative approaches to the admissions problem became ways not of choosing students but of rejecting them without the necessity of meeting them, talking to them, listening to them, and planning with them.

The concern of "higher" education, then, was not with intellectual curiosity, not with self-direction, not with quality of intellectual functioning, not with drive and seriousness of purpose, not with values, but with some convenient techniques for admitting students without the bother of personal attention. The bureaucrats of higher education have succeeded. Their mechanized processes and automated techniques are now standard practices in "evaluating" one's educational preparation. Informed people know that these tests do not really measure the quality of one's education. Yet just about everyone accepts these procedures as ways of controlling admission to college, and practically everyone intimately involved in these processes is vitally interested in the scores which these tests give out. Our leaders, the communities of scholars, have brought us to our present situation.

As the colleges and universities made these decisions about entrance tests and fields of study, the secondary schools of our nation followed along. The elementary programs had to get in step, too. Parents of little children became concerned about the college preparation being given to boys and girls in the primary grades. Parents of high school students demanded that their children be *withdrawn* from honors classes! Why? Because high school teachers were now grading by the standard of restricting high grades to a small percentage of the group. No matter how well qualified *all* of the students in any particular group might be, the number of high grades was limited to a very small percentage. Now if the universities wanted students with high grades, why allow one's child to gamble when the odds were against him? Change his grouping to one in which he would be quite likely to make a high grade. Looked at in this manner, the aim of schooling is obviously not to get a high quality of education. Its aim is to get good grades in order to attend college! Looked at in another way, all of the steps along this rather stupid highway constitute ways of avoiding two central issues: *What is education, and what is teaching?*

What do our elementary (K through 6) schools represent? Are they not really seven years of waiting in order to get into junior high school? And is the junior high school anything more than another three years of waiting in order to get into a senior high school? And isn't the high school another period of detention—three or four more years of waiting before entering college? And isn't college another four-year period of forced detention before one gets a job and the right to live?

And all of this current preoccupation with reading rates! If a student can read faster, he will be able to read more items on the college entrance tests, and if he answers more questions, his score will probably be higher, and if his score is higher, he will have a better chance of getting into the college of "his choice." This is education?

With these ideas as the starting point, we might wish to use our

The Changing Character of Education

imagination and peer into the future. The average length of a school year in the elementary and high schools is 180 school days. The average cost per pupil per year is around $750. Let us pretend that at the beginning of every school day each child must pay his admission fee for the day in cash at the school door. He must hand the teacher four or five dollars, in advance, for the education he will receive that day. But education is now measured by standardized tests, particularly in the field of reading. It is reading that pays off, so it is said. These standardized reading tests report scores in terms of grade level. So a score of 3.2 means that a child is reading at the level of the second month of third grade.

Why not demand of these quantity merchants in education that they make tests which differentiate *daily* achievement in reading? These tests could then be advertised widely in newspapers and magazines and at PTA meetings. There could be repeated programs on commercial TV. These tests could be administered during the last hour of each school day. A child would go home every day with the "objective" evidence that he did or did not get his four dollars' worth of education. Wouldn't that be a wonderful advance in education? And wouldn't it be a remarkably efficient way of evaluating teaching?

Is this a preview of 1984? It could be dangerously close. It is a common practice among teachers in our high schools to drill students on the test items of previous years. There is review and more review. The "proper" subject matter of many high school courses is that content which is closely related to what the college admission fraternity will test for. In other words, education *is* getting into college. That's a simple enough definition, isn't it? Very effective, too. One thus avoids answering this question: What is education? And at the same time, you answer the question: Education is what is needed to get into college.

Millions and millions of dollars were required to bring this whole system into being. Thousands upon thousands of man-hours were needed to get it into operation. Think of the conferences at high levels, the reports of hundreds of committee meetings, the pamphlets, magazine articles, and books that were produced to advance these noble causes. It has all succeeded. The elementary schools have done what the pressures have required, the high schools have emphasized the proper subject content, and the students have been manipulated so that they take the correct number of Carnegie Units. These students have undergone the discipline of the admissions tests, have restrained their dissents, have acquiesced to the standards sets by their teachers, and have said and written what teachers wanted them to say and write. Now the colleges and universities have what they said they wanted.

How Have the Universities Failed?

In one sense, the most cruel of jokes has been played upon the graduates of our high schools. They have prepared for twelve or thirteen years for an educational feast. They have attended "preparatory" schools for years and years; they have studied and crammed; they have obeyed orders and followed directions. They have "adjusted" to the demands of higher learning in America.

Nor have their parents and teachers bothered to think about the meaning of education. When children voiced dissatisfaction with what they were getting, parents told them to "go along with" the system. The system was too big to fight; one couldn't beat it, so one joined it—with the idea that it was only a few more years to college. Then things would be better.

But did things get better? Were the student's needs better met? At the college level did education reflect upon important meanings—the meanings of truth, morality, justice, and beauty? Was education related to issues of the day, to a serious encouragement of dialogue, of dissent, of inquiry into war, poverty, and crime? Are students even now participating in a give-and-take analysis of our social class system, of our industrial establishments and their contributions to the growth of our people, of the violence which now characterizes most of the so-called civilized nations, and especially the violence that is daily revealed in our own culture? What about the role of the blacks in our society? What are some constructive alternatives to possible courses of action, short-term and long-term? Whose vested interests will be hurt or enhanced by each of these alternatives?

Is the college or university the arm of a governing political party of the nation? Is higher education concerned with free and independent inquiry, free from the restraints of political or commercial or religious domination? At the level of higher education do students share in discussions with their professors, in small groups, on matters that really make a difference?

Is the university so organized that in small groupings professors can and do reveal themselves as men of principle, as men dedicated to the enhancement of human living? Is education regarded as a process that involves feelings and emotions, mental and physical health, higher mental processes, and the growth of individual students within their social matrix?

Under the pretext of restricting their emphasis to intellectual concerns, the professors emphasize information and the recall of it. What are the students learning, for the most part? They are again learning how to sit. Presumably, they are learning how to listen, and they are learning all over again how to submit and how to obey the demands of the system. Professors, as a group, are not very interested in the problems of learning, changing behavior, or reconstructing values. They are so busy with their small segment of the departmental offerings that they have little time to delve into the meaning of education and teaching. Moreover, administrators of higher education do not generally reward outstanding teachers. The rewards tend to go to those researchers who are the recipients of outside funds. Rewards often go to those who publish. Why then should faculty members concern themselves with education and teaching?

Professors sometimes defend themselves on all of these counts by saying that they are teaching a discipline. Discipline is that behavior which is consistent with a purpose or purposes. If one of the purposes of the teaching of history is to teach historical methods of inquiry, then students will be disciplined by their own inquiries—that is, by strict attention to the purposes of their research. If practically all of their time is devoted to listening (*not* to active inquiry), they will perhaps be disciplined in listening but they will not have had the opportunity to be disciplined by the methods of inquiry in the field of history. It all depends upon what one means by education.

For many years it has been commonplace to sneer at departments or colleges of education. Most state teachers' colleges are now liberal arts colleges or soon will be. Is there a great difference between the two? Are the sneers justified? As a matter of fact, the difference is between Tweedledee and Tweedledum. One is just as apt to find good teaching in one as in the other. One might find more good teaching at the universities, but this is probably because there are many more teachers there.

You might expect to find many more so-called good teachers in the teachers' colleges, but you won't. Everywhere you go, you will find that teaching is telling and learning is listening. The professor lectures, and the student takes notes; later there are tests. When the term is over, the student has collected some academic credits or points. When he has accumulated the required number of points, he may be certified for a degree. He is now educated; he has been a participant in the process of higher learning. He has been exposed to teaching approved of by the heads of departments, the deans, the executive vice-presidents, and the boards of trustees.

There may be dozens of good reasons why all of this is so. The central and most important reason, as I see it, is that these institutions do not know what they are doing. They have not taken the time to examine their own methods. Most college teachers have little or no preparation for teaching. Most of them have concentrated their studies in a narrow, restricted field and have not had to face up to puzzling questions: *What is education, and what is teaching?*

What are students doing about the university's failings? Right now, and in the recent past, they are rebelling. These are students who are old enough to defend the nation on the battlefields of the world but not yet old enough to carry on a discourse with professors, old enough to make decisions about life and death but not old enough to have some influence in determining their own individualized program of studies, old enough to have gone through the thirteen years of preparation that were demanded but not old enough to share in policy making that deals with curriculum and teaching. In a word, they are old enough to be labeled the next generation but not old enough to participate in the making of it. They are mature enough to know that they are being short-changed, but they are too young to dissent: and they are told to keep quiet, be acquiescent, and go along.

The students have decided to do otherwise, and the faculties, the administrative staffs, and the boards of trustees are shocked. What is really amazing is the patience exhibited by these young people. What is really surprising is that they did not rebel sooner and have not rebelled more often and even more vigorously. Unless there is an intensive exploration of what constitutes an education, and unless teaching receives a critical examination, there will be more revolts. There will be a continuing disrespect for educational authority, which may extend to other authority figures. Our youth beg to be taught. They want an education that concerns itself with meaning. Will they get it?

A most disturbing question intrudes at this point. If all the above is reasonably accurate, how does it come about that the graduates of our professional schools are held in such high esteem both at home and abroad? Their initial selection plays a most significant part. Further, the professional schools encompass much more than an emphasis upon listening and echoing back. But there is a much more important reason.

The real backbone of education in our country is the elementary school. It has been characterized by a reluctance to go along with the "new emphasis" on the memorization of facts and information. Right now it is resisting the computerization of education at the elementary level. It is yielding on the matter of reading in order to read and reading faster in order to read faster. But in general it is holding the line, and it continues its efforts to teach children—your child and mine.

We were extraordinarily blessed in this century with one of the greatest educators of all time, John Dewey. He was concerned with meanings and with the quality of experience which makes up the life of a child. He used his great talents to attack the either–or kinds of arguments which characterize many of the discussions of the issues of our time. He emphasized the relationship of the *means* to the *end.* He was concerned with values, with an emphasis upon thinking. He prized the doubt which helps us to see that we must learn to live with uncertainty. Further, we learn what we live. When the quality of life and living is low and debased, this is what we learn. He helped us all to see that the world continues to be full of unanswered questions and that students should be encouraged to carry on inquiries directed by their own curiosity. In teaching, we must gain a deep respect for the personalities of children. He extolled the values of sharing, one with another, and considered as undemocratic any influence that arbitrarily limits the spheres of interaction with other groups, other peoples, or other races. He had great faith in the use of intelligence and urged a greater use of it in our schools. He believed that thinking comprises action, that ideas are plans of action.

Some of those most interested in Dewey's work have misinterpreted his meaning. Some of the teaching applications attributed to Dewey are far from the mark. In this respect, the fate of his work has been like that of most great leaders. Even so, his work is a landmark. Our elementary schools have been greatly influenced by his teachings. And the very best parts of our entire educational structure are to be found at the extremes: at the elementary school level, and at the level of the professional schools.

2

Awakening Concerns About Teaching

Most encouraging is the awakened concern about the importance of teaching, which has recently begun to manifest itself. The Ohio State University has recently published a document with the title *The Development of a Taxonomy for the Classification of Teachers' Classroom Behavior* (4). This represents a growing concern with what teachers actually do when they teach. The *Yale-Fairfield Study of Elementary Teaching* (1) of 1954-55 also focused upon the activities carried out by elementary school teachers. Intensive study on the work of the classroom teacher is going on in a number of universities: Syracuse, Temple, the University of Illinois, Illinois State University, Teachers College of Columbia University, the University of Michigan, Stanford University, and a host of others have begun studies which hope to throw light upon the question, *What is teaching?*

Ideas of change are in the air, and the speed of this change has accelerated. We are witness to new media of communication. We see the introduction of computers and the changes they are bringing about. Great new technologies have developed within the past twenty-five years. We are exploring space and are planning to land men on the moon. We are transplanting hearts, manufacturing foods, and controlling conception. We are on the threshold of gaining profound insights into the study of degenerative illnesses, the mechanisms of heredity, the activities of the brain.

In all of these ways, and in many others, we are carrying on the scientific revolution begun in the fifteenth and sixteenth centuries. We have created a society in which we are free to inquire, free to experiment, free to doubt, and free to dissent. Freedom is of the greatest value to people *with purpose.* It does not seem to be precious in an atmosphere where people are not self-directing or where they do not prize truth and the pursuit of it.

This liberation of the mind, this repeated *use* of intelligence, has profoundly modified society. There has come to pass not only freedom of inquiry but freedom to communicate one's inquiries: freedom of the press. We have created a society which could not endure without an educated and free citizenry. If the notion of change is the outstanding characteristic of our time, then educators must consider the many ways in which we must educate toward change. This probably means learning how to learn—exerting a more conscious effort to release intelligence. In a world of rapid change it must also mean an increased preoccupation with the ways in which values are developed. A world of rapid change is very threatening to many individuals; their emotional security is weakened. Because of this we must find ways of bringing greatly increased security to learning situations. With the increase in the size of our educational institutions we must find ways of assuring individual contact with every single student, and we must do this in ways which will permit him to learn more about himself and his peers. Several smaller colleges will probably make up the university of the future to give students the opportunity to get to know each other in many ways. Above all, we must do this in a context which cherishes a free and open society, which respects intelligence, and which recognizes the role of tradition and inertia in the face of changing conditions.

THE FUNCTIONS OF TEACHING

In Chapter 3 we shall set forth a comprehensive listing of the ten major functions of the classroom teacher. As we see it, these are the functions of *every* teacher; there are no exceptions. While we are all general practicitioners in the field, we may be teaching only a single subject—mathematics, for example. Yet we come before our students not as mathematicians but as *teachers* of mathematics. And so it is with science or languages, history or fine arts, physical education, vocational education, music, drama, and all the rest.

If you accept the ten components as the major tasks of teaching, does it follow that *every teacher* has an obligation to carry out the ten functions? Let us assume that a science teacher is adept at placing great emphasis upon thinking but does almost nothing that relates to the other nine functions. (It's rather hard to imagine, but let's assume it to be true.) We can say good things about his stress on thinking processes, but what can we say about the remaining functions if he does not discharge them? Does he want the full prestige that goes with being a teacher? Does he want to be on the salary scale with those who discharge all or nearly all of the functions? In terms of these ten components he is *not* a full-fledged teacher. Perhaps he needs help to become one.

Not so long ago, a physical education teacher was a member of a group which was discussing the ten components. He said that the ten functions had little to do with his job, that it was his job to supervise the students while they played games for thirty or forty minutes and to get them back to their classes on time. He added that he prevented any serious fights and saw to it that nearly everyone participated. If a dozen or more physical education teachers had been present, they might have helped him to see the opportunities in his field for thinking, valuing, and developing group power and morale, for meeting some of the emotional needs of the students, for diagnosing, remedying, and showing how, and all the other functions. Surely, physical education teachers as a group would not support him. Do we need another title within our profession for people like this? Or do we want to continue with the present arrangement where he too has the name of *teacher*?

To explore anew our professional responsibilities as teachers is not a pettifogging, superficial inquiry whose primary purpose is to identify a few who should receive merit pay while most of the rest of us remain underpaid for discharging this significant social service. Nor is this inquiry an exercise in rating us as practitioners of the art and science of teaching. As we have looked with doubt and misgiving at the rating systems used for children, so do we also look with suspicion at any enterprise whose primary purpose is to quantify our own professional practices on some scale from mediocre to excellent. What we shall be concerned about are the primary functions of teaching. What do we do when we *teach*? What do we regard as our teaching moments? What expectations do we have of ourselves? Under what circumstances do we experience the satisfaction that we indeed have been teaching?

This approach puts every one of us on common ground with each other. In pursuing this inquiry, we are not fighting each other. We are instead asking: What is the common task of all of us? We know that we differ, one from another. We know that there are probably hundreds of ways of performing our tasks, and all of them might be adequate for the situation. While we are not trying to determine excellence, we are attempting to identify our common tasks and to address ourselves to them.

What do we do when we *teach?*

Formulating a List of Functions

The formulation of a guiding list of functions for the profession of teaching is a task not to be undertaken lightly. Should it be accepted by society, it has the gravest implications for many areas of our national life, let alone the profession of teaching. The present work is the outgrowth of more than twenty-five years of inquiry and the sharing of that inquiry with others.

In its earliest formation the list represented functions which teachers themselves suggested. Their ideas were then mimeographed and shared with hundreds of practicing teachers in the Midwest. The School of Education at the Ohio State University received financial and advisory assistance from the National Commission on Teacher Education to explore in a more systematic manner the functions which were put forth at that time as the central foci of teaching.

Approximately six hundred teachers in the public schools of Ohio agreed to a plan in which each of them would be observed a minimum of *ten* times. Each observation was to be followed by a long interview whose single purpose it was to clarify the significant operations of teaching. Besides these face-to-face interviews with university representatives, these teachers met in small groups of six to ten people to discuss at length what they meant by teaching. There were also regional meetings in which fifty to a hundred teachers were brought together to summarize the outcomes of the individual observations and the results of the smaller meetings. On two occasions all six hundred assembled for a comprehensive summary of what had taken place and what inferences were being drawn from the investigations.

It turned out that the list used in that inquiry was both too general *and* too detailed in its formulations. We also discovered that there was great variability in the acceptance of the total teaching responsibility. At one end of the spectrum there were individuals who wished to limit the teacher's roles to informing, explaining, and showing how. There were expressed and unexpressed fears that the list of functions being studied demanded too much of teachers. Something else emerged that was both troubling *and* satisfying: Teaching is a most difficult,

Awakening Concerns About Teaching 19

most complex series of functions. If one views teaching in terms of the functions to be found in the next chapter, one may agree with many teachers who were in the Ohio project that teaching is indeed a profession. In terms of its demands upon its practitioners, it is probably even more difficult than medicine. This is a humbling thought.

As one might expect, when a number of teachers were brought face to face with the list of functions, they said in effect, "Yes, that is what we should be doing. That is something that is not only desirable but necessary for teachers to do. But where have the teachers' colleges been? Why haven't they prepared us for this kind of functioning?" We did not then have and we do not now have satisfactory answers to this question.

After widespread trial in the Midwest, the list was again revised and mimeographed and tested in the metropolitan areas of New York. Over a period of fifteen years thousands of teachers, some of them graduate students at New York University, examined the document in relation to their own teaching activities. Large numbers of these participants submitted suggestions for rewording, eliminating, and adding functions. Criticisms were sought from the rank and file of teachers. The inquiries were then directed into the suburban areas of New York City and Westchester County, and from there, with the cooperation of Yale University, into southern and northwestern Connecticut. In these new places teachers again responded in terms of their concepts of the profession. Deletions and additions were made, and rephrasings were carried through. The listing has appeared in a number of educational texts. In its various mimeographed forms it has probably had a circulation of at least one hundred thousand copies.

While all of this activity was going on with teachers, it was also possible to present the ideas at Parent-Teacher Association meetings, and this was done on many, many occasions. The ideas were shared a number of times with educational administrators and on one occasion with the Federated Boards of Education of New Jersey. Several educational workshops have been devoted to a searching study of the materials. The most recent trials have been conducted in cooperation with the entire public school system of Roselle Park, New Jersey and with The Middle School of East Orange, New Jersey. The former is an all-white middle class community in which just about half of the graduating high school seniors go to college. The latter is almost one hundred per cent Negro. In both communities the project had the complete support of the administrative staffs and the teachers.

In addition to all of this, there have been the usual public lectures in many states. The University of Wisconsin, at Milwaukee, published one list of functions in a monograph (6) which was the outcome of a series of meetings organized for the express purpose of examining the work of the teacher. The work has been presented before professional colleagues in Maine, Vermont, Georgia, Florida, Maryland, Washington State, California, Kentucky, West Virginia, Tennessee, Delaware, Michigan, Ohio, and New York.

At no time has the material been submitted to the executive officers of the National Education Association. At no time has it been submitted to official representatives of the various state education associations. We have never asked for the approval of associations of administrators or supervisors. The idea, all along the way, has been to have the final product emerge from the interactions of those who are practicing teachers.

We did not solicit the participation of any members of the U. S. Office of Education, nor did we seek the blessings of the highest echelon of the Department of Health, Education, and Welfare. We have stayed away from the official representatives of a great many disciplines. With this publication it now lies open to their critical scrutiny. Not having shared at all in its development, they will have complete freedom to make their assessments of these findings which to a degree affect each of their fields of endeavor.

Is this to be taken as the ULTIMATE, FINAL, AND COMPLETE LISTING of teaching functions? Of course not. Recent reports in the daily press, for example, indicate that before too long we shall have solved the problems associated with tooth decay. Will this influence the work of the dentist, and will this over a period of time bring about changing emphases in the education of dentists? If the stories turn out to be true, it will most surely have a great influence. During the past twenty-five years great headway has also been made with regard to diseases most commonly associated with childhood; this is influencing the emphases in the training programs for doctors. So it will be with teaching, and so it will be with the present list of functions. With the free sharing of our findings and with contributions from fields that may now seem remote, our profession too will advance. On the basis of new experience it will reconstruct its concepts of teaching, and the teacher of tomorrow will be a different kind of practitioner.

How Are the Functions to Be Interpreted?

What about the list at the present time? Is it a *valid* listing of functions of the teacher in today's world? How is validity to be determined in a case like this? As in all cases, the establishment of validity is a social process of longer or shorter duration. With the publication of these materials a process or series of processes will start which will subject the ideas to further serious scrutiny and testing. The ideas will be examined by all kinds of teachers at every level and by all kinds of professional associations.

In other words, the document will enter the public domain for the process of social validation. If it survives and is approved, it may to that extent be regarded as a valid list of functions. If it tends to meet all or nearly all criticisms, if the interacting social influences of each kind accept this material, it can then become a general yardstick for the identification of teaching.

Remember now: it is not a measure of the quality of teaching; it is not a way to rate the teacher. The whole document in its entirety is a way of asking: Does this person simply work in the classroom, or is he *teaching*? Can one relate what is now going on in this classroom, laboratory, workshop, or studio to the functions listed and described in this book?

To bring the point home, let us think for a few minutes about the functions of your family physician when you go in for a physical checkup. What are your expectations of him as a doctor? He probably refers to your health history, which he has recorded previously, and questions you further about events of the recent past. He takes your blood pressure. He listens to your heart. He percusses your chest. He examines your reflexes. He looks at your throat, ears, and eyes. Analyses are made of samples of your blood and urine. These are things he *does*. Thus far, we have not raised the question, *How well does he do them?* We are not attempting to rate him on some scale from zero to a hundred. We may well ask the question, *Is he doing those things which we expect of a doctor in this kind of setting?*

That is precisely the question we are asking about the teacher and about teaching. And practicing teachers themselves have answered the question. They have also said that their answers represent a tall order for the profession. They may be paraphrasing remarks made by the late Senator Robert Kennedy: "We know teachers who dream of things as they are and ask, 'Why?' We dream of things that never were in their entirety and ask, 'Why not?' "

In the processes involved in the development of this form, one could sense again and again the seriousness of purpose of the participating teachers. They seemed to be reflecting an idea once expressed by John Dewey:

> What the best and wisest parent wants for his own child, that must the community want for all its children. Any other ideal for our schools is narrow and unlovely; acted upon, it destroys our democracy.

This means that schools must be evaluated according to the quality of personal, intellectual, and emotional experiences which they provide for their students.

All those who join us in this work of clarifying the functions of teaching must therefore concern themselves with the sort of experience that the child receives at school. With regard to the growing, developing child, what is the quality of experience in the classrooms of our country? What guides the teacher in his functioning? A most important factor is the way in which the teacher's roles are perceived: What is teaching?

And what the teacher does significantly affects the quality of experience. Let us turn now to the present formulation of the major functions of teaching, a first approximation as seen by those who teach and who have shared their ideas with one another. What is the quality of human experience to which these postulated functions give rise?

3

The Ten Components of Teaching

The classroom teacher of today has a thousand and one things to do in order to preserve and deepen the working relationships with children, colleagues, administrators, parents, and lay people. Notwithstanding the multitude of related duties, I will make the attempt here to classify only the *major functions* of teaching. In the process of categorizing, we shall seem to be separating these functions from one another and treating them in isolation. Such a treatment by categorization is inadequate but is done for the sake of exposition. We do not teach by compartments nor do we live in that fashion. We behave as integrated human beings and express a synthesis of many things at any single moment in time. If, however, we are to highlight the major functions, if we are to abstract from the very many things which teachers do those which seem to give a *unique* quality to the teaching profession, we may be forgiven our decision to examine the several aspects of the total responsibility. The *ten* major categories dominating the work of the profession then emerge. These ten functions are requirements for all teachers in all institutions of learning in our society. They are listed, *not* in any order of importance (for they are all important), but as the elements or components of teaching as a whole.

One value of any document such as this lies in the stimulation it might give to all of us to reexamine what we are actually doing as teachers and to clarify for ourselves what we mean by teaching. Any progress we make in this self-searching may be helpful in redirecting the training of teachers in our colleges and universities. We may also be in a better position to contribute to much needed in-service training programs for teachers in our public schools. Still another possible contribution lies in the increased sensitivity which we may bring to the lay public concerning the involved and complex functions required of teachers today. With this increased awareness may come a greatly increased respect for what we are trying to do within the many limitations now imposed upon us.

After listing all ten components, each of them will be treated in greater detail.

Component 1 One very important aspect of the total teaching performance is associated with *informing and explaining.*

Component 2 The tasks of a teacher involve *showing how.* New skills and techniques are often taught in this manner.

Component 3 The existing curriculum and supplies are never completely adequate for every child. Teaching involves *supplementing the existing curriculum.*

Component 4 In our society another requirement of teaching is *to provide opportunities for children to think and share their thinking with each other.*

Component 5 The Teacher is expected *to guide the development of values.* A function of teaching, then, is to provide choices which involve value judgments and give the children opportunities to clarify values and share valuing with each other.

Component 6 The teacher is expected *to relate the life of the community to the work of the school, and that of the school to the community,* with the direct object of enriching both.

Component 7 It is expected that every teacher will do those things which *contribute to a classroom climate in which every student may earn status and respect from his peers.*

Component 8 A new learning situation poses threats for some children. Hence, teachers are expected *to create a relatively secure emotional climate to facilitate learning.* This involves attention to the emotional needs of the individuals who make up the group.

Component 9 A number of children become "behavior problems" at times; a number of children have serious problems in learning and in the normally expected progress of growth and development. Why? Teachers are expected to have trained insights into these matters. They are expected to have the skill to diagnose *difficulties and remedy them.*

Component 10 All teachers are expected *to have competence in evaluating, recording, and reporting* on educational matters of concern, not only to the students in the classroom but to the institution as a whole.

To expect, yes, to require these components of all teachers is indeed a tall order. Even so, we believe that the best and wisest parent *wants* this for his own child, and we believe that an *informed* community wants this for all its children. With guide lines of this nature to direct pre-service and in-service training programs in education, teaching has a sound basis for improving as a profession. And as the profession moves in this direction, it will steadily attract young people with a commitment and dedication to this noble calling.

In addition, as parents interact with teachers whose concerns grow out of teaching as here defined, both will become sensitive to an identity of concerns, and parents will deepen and extend their respect for the profession. In the process, parents will receive a kind of guidance which they sorely need and want. The combined impact of school and home, and of parents and teachers will result in a quality of experience for children that will promote freedom and maturity, individual strength and self-respect, and responsibility and compassion toward others. There will be an increased concern for our communities. Our ideals, our democratic traditions, will have an atmosphere in which they can be sustained and nourished.

Implications of the Components

After reading the list of components or functions of teaching, readers may have questions about what seem to be obvious omissions. The one that is mentioned most often concerns *discipline* or *maintaining order*. We believe that this function is built into the components and that teaching, as here outlined, will forestall most of the problems that are ordinarily associated with the term *discipline*. Component 9 focuses upon the diagnosis and remedying of both learning and behavior problems. Most important, however, is the recognition that discipline is the organization of one's behavior that is consistent with one's purposes. In the long run, it has to mean the acquisition of *self-discipline*—the organization of one's own behavior in ways which will help to achieve success in fulfilling a purpose. Experiences with thinking, valuing, and individual and group responsibilities will do much to minimize the outbreak of discipline problems.

Another frequently made comment about a seemingly obvious omission deals with *motivating students to learn*. And in this instance also, we believe that the requirements associated with motivation are built into the listed set of components. A more complete response to this comment will be found in the extended discussions of each of the components.

A "missing" component, one which maintained its place in the list for a number of years, is *decision making*. It had become a kind of vested interest of its own; its acceptance for many years tended to insure its permanent status in the list. We finally became convinced that practically all of the decisions which teachers make grow out of the ten listed functions. It should be added that the making of these decisions is a most difficult task, and a very frequent one. The decisions which have to be made in "grading" students are practically impossible to make because of the inadequacy of the available data. Many "good, sound, and sufficient" decisions have to be made on the basis of *insufficient* evidence. Another decision that is very difficult to make concerns what content the teacher should emphasize. What knowledge is most worthwhile? And in a time when one national educational organization is pushing one program, another is pushing a second program, and near-by colleges or universities are urging the adoption of still another one, the teacher is very often in a quandary.

The decision not to make a decision is also a judgment. The decision that the situation involves the participation of all those concerned in it is another kind of decision that is sometimes hard to make because of the pressures of time and resources. The decision to refer the matter to some other person or group is also difficult to make on many occasions. The judgment to postpone the decision in certain situations requires a high level of discrimination. All in all, it is a really difficult task to make the many decisions that a teacher faces daily, and often they must be made immediately. Nevertheless, all ten components embody the decision making processes; the practicing teacher carries these functions out when making judgments.

The absence of explicitly stated components concerning *maintaining discipline, motivating learning,* and *decision making* constitute the most frequent comments about omissions.

OBJECTIONS TO THE COMPONENTS

What happened in the seemingly endless discussions of each component in the list? Components 1, 2, 3, 4, and 10 were accepted practically without question as being important and proper functions of every teacher. With regard to the remaining five components there were conscientious objectors to each, and there were some individuals who objected to all five. Some account—overly brief perhaps—will now be given concerning the objections to these five components.

THE TEN COMPONENTS OF TEACHING

1. Informing and explaining
2. Showing how
3. Supplementing the curriculum
4. Providing children with opportunities to think and to share their thoughts with others
5. Helping children to develop values
6. Relating school and community
7. Creating opportunities for each child to earn status and respect among his peers
8. Creating a secure emotional atmosphere to facilitate learning
9. Diagnosing and remedying learning problems
10. Recording and reporting

Component 5

The teacher is expected to guide the development of values. Some objected to the development of values largely upon the basis of the methods suggested for realizing this important objective. More will be said about these methods later when this function is discussed in detail. Some teachers thought that the primary responsibility for the development of values *must* be assigned to the home, that it was not a responsibility of the school as a social institution. Some teachers thought that if it was undertaken as a serious objective, it would open the gates to all kinds of propaganda which teachers who attempted the task would promulgate. Still others thought that we do not know how to develop values and that until we are much more sure of what we are doing we should avoid the responsibility. Some thought that discharging the five components already agreed upon was in itself a herculean task and that the schools should limit their functions instead of expanding them; this line of reason included comments about the pressing time limits that are now imposed upon teachers for "completing" the textbooks assigned to them. There were some who said that it was none of the teacher's business to inquire into the values of his students, that it was a private and personal matter and beyond the reach of teaching.

This detailing of objections may give a false impression. An informed estimate suggests that fully three-fourths of the participating teachers accepted the component as an important and necessary task of teachers in our public schools.

Component 6

Teachers are expected to relate the life of the community to the work of the school, and that of the school to the community. The dissent concerning this component came chiefly from high school teachers. Some saw great difficulties in relating their subjects to community life. Others suggested that if the school became closely involved with the community, it wouldn't be long before the parents would be running the schools. A few agreed with the idea that educational leaders should run the schools and community leaders should run the community. Some thought that the introduction of community concerns was an intrusion into the curriculum and that even without this extra obligation there was not enough time now to give the subject matter at hand the emphasis that it deserved. Others thought of it as a watering down of the educational program. A few suggested that it invited much trouble, because many community concerns involved controversy and it was their notion that a school should not become involved in any way in controversial issues.

Even these relatively few objectors agreed that the high schools should do a great deal with the community through the program of extracurricular activities. But they saw these activities almost exclusively as "displays of the school's excellence" in these areas. High school athletics, high school drama and art, science exhibits, hobby shows, debates, and musical activities were not envisioned as ways of

The Ten Components of Teaching

bringing school and community into closer working relationships. These objectors seemed to fear the idea of closer relationships. It is probably true that in every profession there are practitioners who see their work as a way of escaping from the community and not as a way of participating in it. Over all, there was wide acceptance of this component as a requirement for teaching.

Component 7

It is expected that every teacher will do those things which contribute to a classroom climate in which every student has an opportunity to earn status and respect from his peers. The participating elementary school teachers were practically unanimous in accepting this function as an indispensable component of teaching. Among high school teachers there were a number who challenged this point of view.

Some of them said that the requirement could and should be met by administrative arrangements: a track system with homogeneous grouping within the tracks. They argued that when students were with "their own kind" they would automatically be in a position to earn respect from their peers and that the classroom teacher did not have to do anything about it. And within the track with its homogeneous groupings, a student should earn the respect of his peers in terms of the subject matter offered to his particular group. If he did not, it was too bad, but there was nothing that the teacher should do about it.

They resisted the idea that some recognition might be shown for extracurricular achievement, for example, in a science or math class. A few thought that nothing should take away from the lustre of the subject matter being taught. Some teachers saw little or no need for identifying more closely with the lives of the students, while others thought it impossible to do much individualizing of instruction. A few thought it repugnant to provide students with opportunities to work in areas that interested them most. They saw this as "pandering" to students.

A very few thought that they were *incapable* of doing it well, naturally and gracefully and with real concern, and stated that it would be better not to do it at all, not even to try it, since they lacked the know-how. They wanted none of it and rejected it as a component of teaching. Some of them could not see the significance of students' feelings of personal worth or the relation of these feelings to learning. They saw no real significance in knowing how a student stood with his peers and were even reluctant to talk about the social class stratifications which tend to characterize our culture. "After all," they would say, "this has nothing to do with education."

Such dissent was welcomed, and almost always the dissenters were respected by members of the groups. It was recognized that we differ, that we have a responsibility to present our convictions and share them with others. Name-calling was rare. Every effort was made to relate comments to the aims of education, to teaching, and to the social dilemmas in which we find ourselves. Classroom climate and school morale were recognized as important in the learning-teaching relationships and this component earned a permanent place in the list.

Component 8

The teacher is expected to create a relatively secure emotional climate in order to facilitate learning. Nearly every participant endorsed this generalization as stated. When we began to discuss some of the implications of the statement, we encountered objections but far fewer and less intense than was anticipated. Some teachers were of the opinion that a serious reduction of "fear" in the classroom would weaken the motivations of some of the students. Others thought that there were times when feelings of guilt *should* be intensified; children tended to act or behave better immediately afterwards. The need for praise was widely accepted as a motivating device in learning. Many acknowledged the emotional need to feel that one "belongs" and the need to experience respect and some warm and friendly regard from the teacher, but there was a hint of regret in the admission.

The idea was expressed that one really had to do certain things to facilitate learning with youngsters in individual cases, but that the general idea of "meeting needs" belonged to the home. The home was really responsible for building emotional security. Anyway, if the home situation was indeed bad, the teacher was wasting his time trying to build emotional security in school because the child went home every day to the "same bad situation." To return every day to the "same bad situation" in school was evidently regarded as all right, and particularly so if it parallelled the situation at home.

There were teachers who could not accept the idea that day-by-day attention to these and other needs might be preventive; critical behavior problems could thus be reduced in intensity and frequency. These teachers seemed quite willing to accept the idea that serious behavior problems did arise and that when they did, the involved child should be referred to one of the special services provided by the school.

Throughout the discussions of this component, teachers expressed their awareness of the complexity of the factors entering into the processes of both teaching and learning and with relatively minor reservations they voiced their approval of the function as a vital and necessary part of the total teaching effort.

Component 9

The teacher is expected to have the insight and skills required to diagnose learning and behavior problems and to help children who have those problems. Again the generalization was acceptable, but there were many questions and reservations about the limits of the function and the limitations of teachers. Expressions much like the following were made frequently: "We are not psychoanalysts or psychologists." "We are not experts in this field." "We don't know enough about causative factors." "We have not had the necessary training to do this."

Many teachers said that the pressures of time precluded any serious, sustained attention to any one child and his problems. Some suggested that the school should have many more specialists who would take more or less complete responsibility for all such cases. Underneath all of this, however, there was firm agreement with the idea that where problems interfered with learning, the professional teacher had a responsibility to do everything he could to help. The component received overwhelming support as a necessary component of teaching, and there were hopes that future teachers would be much better prepared to carry out the function.

So much for the most frequently expressed criticisms of five of the components. There were more criticisms, but these are the bulk of those which represent the more serious comments. No attempt has been made to meet the objections, or criticisms in the foregoing summary. In succeeding pages, each of the ten components will be discussed in some length, and in these presentations attention will be given to some of the dissenting views.

4

Components 1-4: Classroom Procedures

Again and again we have raised the question, *What do you do when you teach?* We assume that you are indeed doing *something* when you teach and that others in a position to observe you can recognize and identify this something. We have used the analogy of what the family doctor does when you go to him for a physical checkup. We see him do certain things and perhaps hear him say certain things, but what is going on inside his head at the time, we can only guess. We may not be able to judge his skill as a practitioner or his competence in interpreting the results. Yet later we can say with confidence that he performed a number of functions for us, such as taking blood pressure, looking at eyes, ears, and throat, percussing the chest, and so forth.

One of our aims is to arrive at components which teachers and other observers can easily identify. In attempting this, we have been more successful with some components than with others. We have restricted our aims in two ways: (1) We have limited the spheres of teaching to ten components; that is, the teacher's recall and the observer's attention are *directed*. We are not attempting to be sensitive to a vague notion of *everything*. We are not looking for "personality traits," nor are we looking for "good teaching." *We are searching for teaching itself*, as represented by the ten components or functions.

(2) What does a teacher *do* in a setting designed to give children opportunities to think? Our second restriction is that every component should have observable clues which signify that the component is being carried out. Our thousands of hours (literally) of sharing with teachers assure us that when the teacher is carrying out these operations the teacher knows it, the observer knows it, and there is, practically speaking, *no doubt about it*. If one grants that *providing children with opportunities to think* is indeed teaching, it becomes a relatively easy matter to make the judgment as to whether, in this setting, the teacher is giving students an opportunity to think or not. *The teacher and the observer must both be able to identify the component in the teacher's own actions.*

COMPONENT 1: INFORMING AND EXPLAINING

It is not always an easy matter to distinguish between informing and explaining. In general, *informing* tends to answer questions of who, when, where, what, and questions about procedures and descriptions of things, whereas *explaining* tends to answer the question of why. Both involve the teacher in the process of *telling*.

When he *explains*, he is trying to show the connections between things. It may be a causal relationship. It may be a correlation: if you find one thing, you usually find the presence or absence of another. Almost always the explanation allows for a prediction of future events, and quite often the explanation may be of the kind called "teleological." Why does a cat scratch at the door? Explanation: She wants to get inside. This suggests that something in the future is the cause of something happening now; some scientists and philosophers frown at this kind of explanation. But remember, we are not trying to judge the *quality* of the explanation. Our question with respect to this component is, *Is the teacher informing and explaining?*

Another category of *explaining* which teachers often mention concerns meaning: "I was explaining the meaning of _____." It could be the meaning of the cold war, the meaning of Christmas, the meaning of a term like "juvenile delinquency," the meaning of a direction of study that the class has taken up. In addition to the enlightenment which such explanations offer, children often reveal a sense of satisfaction with the teacher's efforts. That is, one function of an explanation seems to be to satisfy the listener who is receiving it.

The function of *informing* gives the student something which helps him to understand a generalization. He then has some of the facts

Components 1-4: Classroom Procedures

which support that generalization. This function may also inform an interest he has; it may help the student with one of his hobbies. It can relate to a purpose (or attitude, belief, or aspiration) that he has and can modify that purpose. If he wants to become an engineer, the teacher may inform him of the need for studying mathematics. As this procedure is carried on, the students take on informed attitudes, interests, and purposes, and they know what they are talking about when they state a generalization. In other words, the teacher is informing students when what he says is relevant to some enlightenment which the student received.

But we cannot judge how much the students got from the teacher's activities of informing and explaining. Right now, that is not our concern. Was the teacher carrying out the component; was he teaching? The inquiry does *not* deal with the quality or effectiveness of his efforts, nor with his expenditure of effort.

When we ask, "Did the teacher inform and explain?" we are not asking how well he did it, nor are we asking whether the students understood and learned. Rather, we are asking if the teacher performed the function. Did he carry out those activities associated with informing and explaining?

If we can get the answer to this question about each of the components, we can find out what components of teaching are being emphasized in our schools. Then we shall see more clearly what we are doing and will be in a better position to change our emphases, if that is desirable.

COMPONENT 2: SHOWING HOW

From pre-school through high school, every teacher in our samples accepted the function of *showing how* as one of the very important functions of a teacher.

In carrying out the task of showing how, the teacher should realize that there is no one perfect way of demonstrating "everything." As with explaining, the complexity of the learning task is a factor and the previous preparation of the students is another. Language barriers may operate to hinder instruction, and the resources for demonstrating may be inadequate. The standards employed for judging the work of students may also influence the entire process of *showing how*.

The teacher almost always does the demonstrating. Often, he does it over and over again until the large majority of the group seems to comprehend it. Sometimes he asks other people to do the *showing how*—it may be students within the group, former students, or an adult from the community. Sometimes it may be another teacher.

In this context, showing how *always* means that children are expected to learn the skill that is being demonstrated. It does not mean, for example, telling children how photosynthesis takes place. That surely involves informing and explaining, but it is not something that children can learn how to do. If a teacher is carrying out this function of *showing how*, he must not only see to it that the demonstrations are carried out before the group but he must also give ample time for the children to practice the processes until they have arrived at an acceptable degree of control. Very often this involves a great deal of patience and understanding about how children learn.

Two factors must therefore be present before we can affirm that the teacher is *showing how*. One of these involves the idea of *demonstrating*—in a variety of ways, including movies and film strips if they seem appropriate. The second vitally necessary factor is that the students have *ample time to practice* what has been demonstrated, and do in fact practice it.

The second point deserves a great deal of emphasis. Without always being aware of what they are doing, many teachers in our junior and senior high schools tend to shorten the time for practice, the time for *learning how*. To learn a skill, to acquire some mastery of it, children must do the required actions. How much practice time is enough? This can only be answered by the teacher in charge of the group. One very poor answer to the question characterizes the work of some teachers; they seem quite satisfied when about half the class has learned how. If the genuine aim is to show the class, then just about everyone in the class should learn how, and the teacher should stay with the project until this goal is reached.

The Importance of the Teacher's Values

Repeatedly within these pages, we have pledged ourselves to present and discuss what the teacher does—*not* how well he does it. We made no such promises about discussing problems or difficulties in carrying out the components. There is a widespread notion that teaching is easy, that just about anybody can teach, and that a few slogans or adages will carry one through: "You have to show 'em who's boss in the first few days." "You have to keep 'em busy, always busy." "Speak softly, but let them all know that you carry a big stick. Discipline should be hard and firm, because more than anything else students have to learn to obey." "If the children are enjoying themselves in school, if they are quite happy as they are learning, there must be something wrong with the program because good education is supposed to be hard and painful." "You catch more flies with sugar than with vinegar." "A good teacher runs a tight ship. She doesn't live *with* children; she always dominates them. First and foremost, she's the boss: she decides right and wrong, good and bad, truth and falsity, just and unjust, and her decisions are *absolute*, not to be questioned." In these circumstances children are not people; they are receptacles into which the teacher pours information and his own value judgments.

Taking the two components thus far presented—*informing and explaining* and *showing how*. They represent two difficult arts and skills of the profession which test the powers of the teacher to communicate with students. It is very necessary to use language that is appropriate to the age level, to use examples that are within the experience of those in the class. It is necessary to tie up the new with the old in their life's span. In this dynamic process the teacher is almost continually noticing the facial expressions of the children with whom she is communicating. He is sensing the appropriateness of what he is saying and doing, makes the necessary repetitions, modifies these repetitions in such a way that they do not seem repetitive, and thus decreases the chances of boredom. He doesn't over-explain, or under-explain. Real distinction in the art derives from the teacher's ability to offer just enough to meet the needs of the situation.

The *informing* aspect of Component 1 is no less subtle. Informing a student is quite different from "re-forming" him, and the distinction between these two must be clear. When *informing* takes on the qualities of rigidity and dogmatism, the children are not participants in a program of learning. Instead, they are receivers of information. When the teacher informs students, he awakens interest in the usefulness of the information, calls forth any questions that might be in the minds of the students, and asks if any of them want to expand upon or interpret what has been presented. In other words, he is sharing information with students and inviting them to respond. He is not merely "handing out" facts to be learned.

Similarly, *explaining* is not always the simple function it is assumed to be. We have not always explained something when we have told the students our own comprehension of the matter. On many occasions the art of explaining must be imbedded in a context which is reassuring to the students. Explanations are offered with the hope of *acceptance*. This quality of acceptance is not identical with the logic of the explanation, it is associated with the security of the person who is receiving the explanation. The skilled and experienced teacher is aware of this necessary ingredient. When he encounters obstacles along the way, he is alerted to the presence of elements that might be taken as threats to the security of the student. Using this context is a high art which a great many of our teachers possess. And along with it there is the need for informed patience, for the consideration of individual differences, for variations in methods of presentation, for providing the space, the tools, and the materials for learning. And for nearly all of us who teach, it involves careful preparation ahead of time. Parents and lay people generally should come to know how very difficult it is to teach. Success in the task and continuing improvement in discharging these two functions probably depend largely upon a continuing self-examination by the teacher of what he is doing.

COMPONENT 3: SUPPLEMENTING THE CURRICULUM

Professor Howard Lane at New York University once said that if a teacher wanted homogeneous groups and wanted them to stay that way, the best approach would be to arrange these homogeneous groups on the basis of weight. In practically all other ways every group of children (or men or women) is characterized by a great many differences. One of the reasons for supplementing the curriculum is to try to provide for these differences. A second important reason is to guard against the boredom that seems to accompany the day-by-day use of the same texts and the same workbooks for every child in the class. Whenever the teacher notices that the text treats a topic sparingly, he may supplement it to add richness and meaning to the course of study. Some math texts may prove to have inadequate practice materials; if students need more practice, it becomes necessary to supplement the text. On occasion there is a topic that is not treated at all in the text. If a teacher wants to take advantage of unexpected and unplanned episodes, or topics in the news, there is a need for supplementing the curriculum. When one is alive to the needs of the learners and sensitive to the limitations of the standard text materials, there are many opportunities for enriching the curriculum, for making it more effective for all students.*

If there is an observer in the room, one who is sensitive to these teaching components, what are some of the things he might see when the teacher is supplementing the curriculum? He might observe that

---

*See also the implications for modifying the curriculum in the discussions of other components.

a) every student is not at work on the same task, that individuals or small groups within the class are working on different materials;
b) slides, film strips, movies, tape recorders, and overhead projectors are in use;
c) students are actually using newspapers and magazines as sources of information;
d) students are using paperbacks (and again different children would be using different ones);
e) students are using a variety of reference books;
f) differentiated assignments are given out, even if the same text is being used;
g) the children and teacher have been on a field trip or are planning to take such a trip;
h) some idea or story is going to be dramatized: a script is being composed and various kinds of resources are being used;
i) various kinds of 'collections' are being utilized: stamps, coins, picture postcards, insects, weaving, or pottery;
j) visiting speakers are present, if they are in the room sharing their ideas with the children;
k) children are sketching or painting scenes that are relevant to what is being studied;
l) the teacher is using his own testing materials;
m) the teacher is using his own mimeographed materials, which put an emphasis upon thinking and values;
n) the teacher and students planned to watch a TV program at home and the group is now discussing it; and
o) the teacher and the children may be using some of the most recently developed supplementary materials and devices: programmed instruction, learning and teaching machines, and videotape recorders which can play back tapes for the students.

The list of possibilities seems to be endless. Because this component of *teaching* is almost immediately identifiable, any informed observer would recognize when the classroom teacher is supplementing the curriculum. It is an indispensable role of the teacher. Here again, we have not raised the question of how well he does this supplementing. Rather we have asked: Is the teacher doing this? If he is, he is teaching.

COMPONENT 4: PROVIDING OPPORTUNITIES FOR STUDENTS TO THINK AND TO SHARE THEIR THINKING

Several colleagues and I have published a book on this component, entitled *Teaching for Thinking* (8). It contains hundreds of illustrations of ways to emphasize thinking in classroom work. One section is directed to teachers who are working with children who have not yet become fluent readers, while there is another section designed for use by teachers in the upper elementary grades and still a third part intended to be helpful to high school teachers. The book has been widely acclaimed and is useful for teachers who wish to fulfill this component of teaching.

What would an observer see taking place in the classroom if teachers were providing opportunities for children to think and to share their thinking?

a) He might see students in the act of *observing and listening, feeling and smelling, tasting, and reporting sense impressions*. As they share the results of the assignment with others in the room, they would be learning that we all do not see, hear, feel, smell, or taste the very same things. We differ. Sometimes we become more alert to what others are sensing and more discriminating as a result of this sharing process. Moreover, we almost never report *everything* we have sensed; we select what to report and give emphasis to some things.

b) The observer may see children in the act of *comparing two or more things*. The objects for such comparison may be drawn from quite a diversified list. They may be two pets that are in the room, two leaves, or two trees. They could be two toys or two automobiles, two pictures or two short stories, two pieces of music or two poems. Two translations of the same paragraph from a foreign language, two mathematical proofs, or two similar scientific experiments. Large concepts might be the focus of such comparisons: classicism with romanticism, an early work of an author with one of his later works, modern music with modern art, or the scientific philosophy of the seventeenth century with that of the eighteenth century. There is practically no limit to the topics and ideas which might be compared. The task of comparing and contrasting affords the student an opportunity to do some thinking.

c) In *summarizing*, children must abstract the major points and consolidate them into a briefer formulation; this requires thinking. An appropriate assignment might involve summarizing a movie that has been shown, or a field trip, or a filmstrip. The students might be asked to prepare a summary of a short story or a book, of their vacation, or of a TV program. Here again there are a great many opportunities which a teacher can use to emphasize this thinking operation.

d) *Classifying* also gives children an opportunity to think. In their very earliest years children may be sorting blocks or arranging beads. Older children can classify books, games, or clothing styles. Lists of words and phrases might be classified according to parts of speech. Again, a list of cities, countries, or rivers might present the challenge to organize and classify. Any task of this sort calls for thinking.

e) *To interpret or to find meaning in an experience* is the result of some thinking about that experience. For the teacher to give a table of data or a graph to a student and ask, "What meaning does this have for you?" is to give that student a chance to think. To interpret one's own experience requires thinking. To delve into the possible meanings of a poem, a picture, a drama, a dance, or a scientific discovery is to take an opportunity to think. The practical arts abound with such opportunities, and much the same can be said about every subject in the curriculum.

f) The students may be trying *to solve problems* of one kind or another—problems in mathematics or science, or shop or laboratory problems.

g) Students may be confronted with situations which test their ability *to make decisions*. This is not a question of what is the correct answer; it may simply determine what is the wisest decision to make in a given situation. Students are asked to give reasons which support the preferred alternative. In sizing up alternatives, considering the interests of all concerned, and anticipating consequences, genuine opportunities to think arise.

h) Giving students an opportunity *to use their imagination* in order to visualize the future or the very distant past is to give them a chance to think.

i) *Looking for assumptions* is another activity which involves thinking. It is usually motivated by a searching and critical analysis of some conclusion. It asks these questions: Has it been absolutely proven? If we 'swallow' this conclusion, are we also taking for granted something that has not been mentioned? What else must we also believe if we accept this conclusion?

j) Students may be at work on a large project—one involving several weeks of work and entailing the use of the library, the writing of letters to specialists, and perhaps interviewing, poll-taking, or making and administering a questionnaire. It involves the planning of time and often involves committee and group work. *To put large projects into operation* is to give students many opportunities to think.

k) When students are faced with some of society's unsolved problems and are asked *to suggest hypotheses for possible solutions*—to have 'hunches' about ways of tackling the problems—they are learning to think. The problem could be one of public apathy about juvenile crime, small voter turn-outs, traffic accidents at particular times or places, or weather predictions. It might deal with anything from increasing local income or decreasing taxes to drop-outs or drugs. In every subject area there are problems that have not been solved; students can learn from such endeavors.

l) When students as a group have a chance to talk about problems they would like to work on, the teacher may list all of the suggested possibilities on the blackboard. From this list each student may choose one and reformulate it in his own words. *Collecting facts and organizing them in terms of one's own purposes* requires thinking.

m) The classroom observer may see and hear students in the process of *evaluating or criticizing* something. This involves the identification of both strengths and weaknesses of whatever is being scrutinized. When students are required to give a basis for their comments, to demonstrate the relevance and the reasonableness of their judgments, they are involved in the processes of thinking.

n) When reading the written work of students, some teachers employ a technique called *coding*. If a student uses such words and phrases as *all, every, never, none, the best,* or

Components 1-4: Classroom Procedures

the poorest, then the teacher places an X in the margin. He explains that the symbol means that an 'extreme' word has been used. He does not mark it incorrect but simply calls the student's attention to his use of the word. If after giving some thought to the problem the student states that he does not want to change it, that it seems to him appropriate in the particular context, then the teacher accepts his decision. The coding symbols used vary with teachers and the kinds of expressions coded also vary. Some teachers code the word *or*, thus helping the student to see that he has oversimplified some problem into an *either-or* analysis. Sometimes qualifying words or phrases are coded, such as *it seems, I feel, it appears, perhaps, maybe, possibly, might, could,* and so on. This is done to bring to the attention of the student his patterns of word usage or repetitions of words. Symbols are sometimes used to identify value judgments and if-then statements, to call attention to generalizations, similes, analogies, or metaphors, to point out name-calling or labeling, assumptions of cause and effect, and attributions of positive and negative kinds. When required to defend what he has written, when required to reexamine his judgments, the student is put into a position where thinking is required.

o) After some experience with examining their own coded papers, students are sometimes assigned the task of *coding the writings of others*. They may be given excerpts from newspapers or magazines, possibly a 'letter to the editor'; research reports, short stories, writings of many kinds.

This listing does not pretend to be complete. There are a great many ways of providing students with opportunities to think. The ones presented include only the common practices among teachers who put an emphasis upon thinking.

To get back to the main point, if any of these processes are going on in the classroom, an observer can not mistake them. He would know that they are going on and that the teacher was giving students *opportunities to think*. If one accepts this component, then one would have to say that this teacher is teaching.

5

Components 5-6: Relating to the Outside World

COMPONENT 5: HELPING STUDENTS TO DEVELOP VALUES

With the help of colleagues, I have written a book about this component, *Values and Teaching* (9). In this volume one will find discussions of the meaning of values, the ways they are expressed, the ways teachers stimulate the expression of values, and the ways he might most effectively react to value-type expressions.

Values are those influences which give direction to our lives. Such values begin to operate when an opportunity to make a choice among the known alternatives comes along. They represent our own free choices—not the demands, hints, or suggestions of others. We sometimes think that they originate in our 'conscience,' and so we prize and cherish them if they are *our* values, we are proud of them; they lead us to make certain choices. Values influence the ways we spend our time and money, and they have something to do with our choice of friends and acquaintances. They are the ideas that we will stand up for. When we have values, they are very important in guiding our lives.

When students talk about their hopes, aspirations, desires, or purposes, they are making value-type statements. When they are sharing

45

their feelings, attitudes, beliefs, and interests, they are also making value-type statements. When they talk about their worries, concerns, or problems, almost always such statements involve values. When they talk about what they would like to do over the weekend or during the summer, and so forth, quite probably *they are sharing value-type statements with those who are listening.*

The first point then in helping children to develop values is to *give them an opportunity to talk about their life experiences*—to set the stage in such a way that value-type expressions will come out into the open. An observer present in the classroom will have little or no difficulty identifying this process if it is going on.

Secondly, the teacher has to listen and demonstrate that he has listened to the value-type expressions. Having set the stage for the performance, having asked the students for their reactions, it becomes absolutely necessary *to listen and react.*

Before talking about ways of reacting, we must go back again to the roots of values: Where do they come from? It seems fair to assume that they arise out of our own uniquely personal life experiences. They represent an interpretation, *our* interpretation, of *our own* life experiences—not any single experience in isolation, but our totality of living. Anyone who criticizes our values, our attitudes, or our interests is criticizing our life. The particulars of our life may not mean much to others, but it is the only life we have had, and generally we prize it and want others to show respect for it.

In other words, as teachers, we cannot assume that our attitudes are *the correct ones* and that the attitudes of the students are *wrong.* If the student has said something that is consistent with his life experience, he has uttered a sincere attitude. For him to say something contrary to his own personal life would be hypocritical. We may wish that his life experiences had been otherwise, but we cannot say of his life that it is a true or a false life. And we cannot say that his hopes, desires, wishes, or aspirations are correct or incorrect attitudes. We cannot say that he has the "wrong" feelings or the "wrong" interests or concerns. They are his; they represent his life. What then can we do?

Do we accept everything? Almost everything, but there are a few very important exceptions. First, we restrain any and all activities which represent an immediate danger to the life and health of the students. Second, we reject extreme vulgarity. If the student is unaware of what he is saying or doing, we might indicate that we will talk with him privately about it. Third and last, we should be sensitive to a very few local taboos, issues which the neighborhood or

Components 5-6: Relating to the Outside World

town regards with distaste (or even horror) because of the feelings of the people involved. Should students venture into these domains, with all the tact we possess we should endeavor to change the subject, to fly away to another safer comment, or to indicate the need for postponing the discussion of it.

Let us recap what has been said thus far about the teacher's observable activities in carrying out this component, *helping to develop values*:

1. The teacher creates the situations in which students feel free to express and do in fact express attitudes, interests, feelings, purposes, aspirations, beliefs, worries, and concerns which *they* have.
2. The teacher listens and (with a few exceptions) accepts and respects what has been said.

A third kind of action on the part of the teacher is now required. *He interacts with the student.* He responds to what the student has said and does so with one single, governing purpose: he wants the student to be consciously aware of what he has said in order to stimulate him to do some reflection on it. That's all there is to it, but it is a most important function. Think of the few links in this chain. Imagine what it must mean to any student who becomes involved in it. "My feelings have been asked for. Evidently, they are regarded as important. (I am important; my life is important!) What's more, the teacher has listened to me and has respected me. To have someone just *listen* is wonderful. What's more, he has asked me a question or two which have set me to thinking about my feelings. He has taken me seriously. I wish this could happen to me more often!" So say we all.

Interacting With Students

How does the teacher interact? The ways are legion. In the book previously mentioned, *Values and Teaching*, thirty suggestions are made about things to say and questions to ask which challenge the student to do some thinking about what he has said or done. In any case, the teacher should use only one or two of these at a time; he should *not* carry on a protracted public interview with the student. The encounter or transaction is very brief. After making one or two questions or statements, the teacher accepts the student's responses with such comments as "I see what you mean," or "Now I understand it more clearly," or "Let's talk about this again some time," or "Interesting point of view!" These are only a few of the ways in which the teacher may close the short colloquy in order to turn to something else.

The thirty suggested ways of interacting all have one very important quality: The student to whom they are addressed is *the only person* in the world who has the answers to the questions or comments made by the teacher. They deal with *his* life, *his* views, *his* feelings, *his* attitudes. If the questions or statements bear upon these facets of *his* life, *he alone* can answer them. In this brief but magnificent moment he is the center of the universe. The teacher—*his* teacher—has accomplished all of this in a minute or two in the classroom setting. Miracle of miracles! The teacher will do it again and again with many students. He will be doing it as part of an inescapable and highly prized function of his professional life in teaching. Moreover, as he does it, he doesn't make a $64,000 issue out of the interaction. He does it casually—with the left hand, so to speak—Much like that doctor who has taken your blood pressure in the setting of doing a physical checkup. The doctor doesn't give you the impression that attaching the instrument to your arm is a matter of life or death at the moment. It is just a part of the process of the total physical examination. In much the same way, the teacher carries forward the processes of clarifying and stimulating some thinking about value-type statements.

Here are some of the thirty suggested ways of interacting with the students:

a) *Are you saying that———?* or *Is this what you mean?* (and then paraphrasing what the student has said)
b) *Could you expand on that? I'm not getting your meaning.*
c) *Could you give us an example of what you mean?*
d) *Does this attitude* (purpose, feeling, etc.) *mean a great deal to you?*
e) *Do you think our society would be better off if most people agreed with you? In what ways?*
f) *Does what you say represent a minority opinion, or is it a majority perhaps? What evidence is there for this opinion?*
g) *What would be an opposing belief?*
h) *Are you assuming that———?*
i) *What is good about an attitude of this kind?*
j) *What sorts of experiences have you had which might have led to the acceptance of this attitude?*

A great many more exist. In any context only one or two of the many ways are utilized. We have assumed an oral context but much

Components 5-6: Relating to the Outside World 49

the same thing could be done as the teacher reads what the student has written. When the teacher encounters a value-type statement, he can write a question in the margin. We make the assumption that if a student has to examine again what he has said or written, and if he is asked a question or two about it, he will see more clearly what he does believe. This introduces the student to the process of developing his own values. Such day-after-day, month-after-month self-confrontation in an atmosphere of acceptance and security constitutes the discipline of self-discovery. As teachers, we may not be doing an earth-shaking job at any one encounter. But such steady emphasis reveals our own prizing of informed beliefs, informed purposes, informed interests, and the student grows in maturity as he comes to see who he is and what he stands for in a variety of contexts.

Eliciting Values

Thus far we have said very little about ways of eliciting value-type statements from a class. As a number of ideas are shared with teachers, they usually add to such a list. The teachers come to recognize situations which have potential for the revealing of value-type sentiments. Such value-eliciting statements follow; some are much more appropriate for younger children, and some for those who are older.

a) If you had all the power in the world, or if you were a great magician and could change the world, what would be the very first change that you would make? The second?
b) If you had a hundred dollars given to you for your very own, how would you spend it?
c) What is more important? To have friends? To have money? To have libraries? Why?
d) You see four people who are in great danger. One of them is an artist, one is a scientist, one is a businessman, and one is a man who builds houses. You are able to save *only one* of them. Which one would you try to save? Why that one?
e) Of all the very famous men or women whom you have heard about, which one of them would you like to be? Why?
f) Suppose you could choose between living in some far-off time of long ago and living in our very own present time? Which would you choose? Why?
g) Tell about some experience that made you
   1) very happy,
   2) very sad,
   3) very excited,

      4) very tired,
      5) very bored, etc.
h) Tell us how the world will be one hundred years from now.
i) In regard to some current news event as reported on TV or radio or in the press, what is your reaction to this story?
j) What are some of your reactions regarding a movie that has been shown, a story or poem that has been read, a piece of artwork that has been seen, or music that has been heard?
k) What are some things that get on your nerves, or tend to make you a bit angry?
l) What are some things that scientists have done which in your estimation are not good?
m) Take your time and prepare a statement giving your reactions to one of the following:
      1) The armed services should draft women.
      2) Transplanting the heart of one person into the body of another person is not a moral or religious issue.
      3) Everyone should receive free medical care.
      4) Education should not be compulsory.
      5) Whether a person works or not, he should get a certain guaranteed income.
      6) Divorce should not be allowed, or else it should be much easier to obtain a divorce.
      7) Anyone who drives an automobile should be compelled to take a physical examination every year; if he doesn't pass, he should not be allowed to drive.
      8) Boys and girls should have the right to vote when they are 18 years old.
      9) Students should be taught much more about the history of Negroes.
     10) Art should be a *required course* for every student in every grade, including high school.
     11) It's rather silly to study foreign languages; before long, everyone will be using English.
     12) If young people do something that is very wrong, they should be punished for it, *and* so should their parents and family.
     13) What's good and what's bad about TV?
     14) All of us, perhaps at some time in our lives, have told "fibs," white lies. Some people lie outrageously. What is so bad about this? What are some of the most important reasons for telling the truth?
     15) It has been said, "It is better that one hundred guilty men shall go free, than to find one innocent man guilty for a crime he did not commit." What do you think of this?
     16) What are some of the things about our society which you believe are in dire need of correction?

Components 5-6: Relating to the Outside World

The list could go on and on. Such questions elicit the reactions of students. As they respond, attitudes and beliefs come tumbling out; concerns are revealed; the hopes and desires of students become evident and the teacher has a chance to listen and to interact.

We started with the question, *Is the teacher helping students to develop their own values?* We have indicated that three kinds of behavior have to be present when he is carrying out the component:

1. He has created a situation, or many situations, in which students can reveal their concerns;
2. He listens with respect and accepts his students when they express their own feelings; and
3. He interacts with the students in ways that lead to self-examination and to awareness of what one stands for.

We submit that these operations are recognizable to the eyes and ears of the observer and can easily be discerned if they occur as comments on the written papers of students. When these three activities are being carried forward, the teacher is helping to develop values.

COMPONENT 6: RELATING SCHOOL AND COMMUNITY

There is an old, old saying to the effect that, when teaching, "you have to start where the children are." Like many old sayings, it is at best a half-truth. As a teacher, you start where the children are *and where you are*—in the community. The community is the children's home, but despite that fact, they often know very little about it. If a teacher knows even less and cares almost nothing about the community, this will be reflected in the ways he interacts with the students.

There is another commonplace expression to the effect that "where you find good schools, you also find a good community." Does this mean that schools add to the value of a community? Or does it mean that a good community is likely to have good schools? Does it mean that a good community is very careful about the employment of school personnel—principals, teachers, special service people, and the superintendent? Or is it all just a question of money? In the so-called good communities the pay is better, the parents are willing to pay higher taxes for buildings, supplies, and equipment, and hence the schools are better. Does this suggest, if you were to take any community and raise everyone's salaries tonight by a very significant amount, that the next day the whole staff would be much more effective? Very few people, including teachers, would agree that this would be so.

Some people sum up their views by saying that a community gets the schools that it deserves. This whole matter is actually a two-way street; it is the *relationships* between school and community that are decisive. The community itself is tremendously significant; its culture, its life, its vitality, its concerns, and its hopes and aspirations are crucial. Even so, if the school does not respond, it will not be long before the community begins to reflect this lack of concern about the many factors which relate to teachers, teaching, and learning.

When the *relationships* between school and community deteriorate, one is more apt to find that school budgets are rejected and school bond issues fail. The public meetings of the board of education reveal bitter criticisms of individual principals or teachers, or criticisms of the schools as a whole. There may be an unusually high turn-over in the teaching staff each year. There may be frequent changes in administrative personnel and there will be a tendency to cut down on supplies and equipment that are greatly needed. At home children will hear conversations that reveal disrespect for teachers, principals, and the school program. Morale falls sharply.

Whose fault is it? When the bottom is reached and the situation is about as bad as it can be, scapegoats are sought and found. A relatively detached observer sees quite clearly that *everybody* is to blame, as is almost always the case in such "bad relationships." In such a time teachers sense the need for a united defense. Through local and state associations or through teachers' unions, they begin to fight back. Almost always these developments emphasize salaries of teachers, extra pay for extra work, procedures for negotiating with the board, tenure, dismissal processes, and things of a like nature.

The community leaders seldom tackle the problem of deteriorating relationships. They howl about the budget or the administrators, or perhaps about reading, spelling, or arithmetic. The teaching personnel respond by avoiding the central problem of "poor relationships" and by substituting for it matters of salary, tenure, and others. The frustrations of the teachers and the community leaders lead to bitter and hostile expressions that make the *relationships* even worse. Sometimes it takes many years before it is all straightened out again. And due to the nature of all very deep-seated quarrels, the community may never really regain its original status.

Sometimes we recognize the irrationality of all this and we say that, had certain things been done long ago, "this never would have happened." What are these things? What constitutes that component of teaching which deals with the relationships of the school to the community?

Alone, unaided, we teachers know that we cannot do the complete job of educating children. The community educates in most significant ways. We know that there has to be a cooperative relationship between us and the parents and the community as a whole. We have pretty much the same concerns for the children, for their present and their future. We know that each family is a unit in the community and that the interrelationships of these families constitute the community. We know also that a student is a child of a family and that when he comes to school, he brings his family and its life along with him. That is, when he comes, he brings a certain portion of the community.

We teachers are also a part of his community. We get our salary from community funds and make use of various community resources. In small or large measure we mingle with some of the people in the community and make the community what it is. If we can say that a child brings to school certain ideas about his community, we must also acknowledge that after being with *us* four or five hours, he also takes home some of our ideas about his community. He brings and he takes. What does he take from us? What do we offer him? What do we *do* that impinges upon the relationships between the community and the school?

The Family and the School

Let us begin by acknowledging that *the family* is the basic unit of the community. If we start strong relationships with families, we shall have started the process of relating school to community. Does the classroom have one large bulletin board reserved for family affairs? Are there pictures of each child's family shown? Are there pictures of fathers and mothers at their places of work? Are there pictures of family pets, or family trips and outings?

Is there a map of the school neighborhood with all the streets showing, and is the location of each child's home shown on this map? When news of a family appears in the local paper and is appropriate for sharing, is it clipped and placed on the bulletin board? If a child is absent for several days, do the teacher and students get in touch with the family to see what may be wrong? In a number of ways, does the teacher let the family and the child know that he is missed in school and that the class hopes he will be back soon? If there is a death in the family, are there ways in which the teacher and children can show their sympathies? If one member of a child's family has been away from home for some time—at college, working in another city, at a convention, or on a pleasure trip—is this known, and are such "outsiders" sometimes asked to come in and share their experiences with the group?

Perhaps the family bulletin board contains information about the interests and hobbies of the parents. These often represent valuable resources for the further education of the children. Many parents know far more about some things than teachers do and have unusual skills to share with the children. Collections which they have may be on exhibit in the room. Almost always these interests cover a wide span and are usually unknown to the teacher.

In almost every room there is a child whose family has lived in the community for several generations. They are extremely well informed about the history of the community. If one of them can be persuaded to come in and talk to the children about "old times," they may point out some of the significant changes (from their personal point of view) that have taken place in schools, industry, housing, family entertainment, roads, stores, playgrounds, and many other things. Wherever there are people, one usually finds some who write, some who sing or play musical instruments, some who draw, paint, or sketch, some who are entertainers, and on occasion all are willing to come and share their talents. Perhaps some of this sharing can be done in the evening, too.

We are still talking about ways of relating ourselves to the community, in this instance, to the families of the community. The ways we treat *each* student are very important in terms of cementing community-school relationships. Do we give help where it is needed? Do we respect each student? Are we fair and just in our treatment of students? Are we patient with their stumbling efforts to learn? Or do we give rewards to a favored few? Do we get angry at a certain few of the students whom we consider "troublemakers"?

In common practice there is not very much communication between school and home, between teacher and family. There is, however, one point of contact whose significance we often overlook. In every instance when a student takes home work which he has done in school, that piece of work and the teacher's comments on it represent the school to the parents. With how much care was the work reviewed by the teacher? What did he have to say about the student's efforts? About his progress? Were his positive accomplishments noted, or did the teacher only point out the errors?

Some teachers make it a point to send notes home rather frequently. Some are mimeographed statements which describe the

Components 5-6: Relating to the Outside World

work being done in one or more subjects. Some are commendations of the work of an individual child. Some are invitations to visit a particular session or series of sessions. Some tell about an assembly program, an art exhibit, or a school "sing." All of them reveal a concern about the family's stake in the work of the child. We may not always realize it, but to his family a child is a highly prized individual. What touches him touches the family. A teacher whose "eagle eye" is forever looking for mistakes, for shortcomings in behavior, for defects in character, who almost never has anything good to say about children, is not establishing the very necessary cooperative relationships between school and community. When these relationships are bad, learning suffers. The child is educated not only in the school; he is also educated by his family, his peers, and his community.

Make no mistake about it. This is *not* image-building alone; this is not false, stuffy public relations blah-blah. Moreover, it is *not* pandering to the child or his parents. This is the stuff of building a solid relationship between school and home, a relationship that fosters learning of many kinds.

Many things have been mentioned in connection with the central role of the family. A classroom observer looking around the room can note immediately if matters of family concern are prized in that room. As he listens to what the teacher says and does, as he listens to the children's questions and comments, he will know in a rather short time whether the teacher, the teaching, the learners, and the curriculum are in any way family-oriented. The teacher herself knows when her work as a teacher puts emphasis upon family relationships.

Taking the School Into the Community

School-community relationships are also strengthened when children and teachers go out into the community for field trips, for fun, for pleasure and recreation, and for rendering a professional or community service. Some teachers give talks to various local clubs or associations, while others make it a point to go to some of the community concerts or plays. Some teachers occasionally attend board meetings or court trials, go to a number of different churches, or visit a hospital to know the conditions there. Some visit the playgrounds, swimming pools, and picnic areas to get some idea of the availability and quality of these local resources. There are also the trips into the community in which the teacher is ordinarily the leader. Many times a small group of parents go along to assist. The whole trip is usually planned in advance; there are discussions of time, route, special things to look out for, questions which should be asked, ways in which the newly acquired experiences will be summarized upon return to the classroom. Sometimes a trip is planned in terms of an opportunity for comparison and contrast: two factories are visited, or two municipal centers, or two neighborhoods. The children are asked to be alert to ways in which the two are alike and ways in which they are different.

In one community that we know of, the school appointed committees of children to keep track of several entire blocks within the school district. On the positive side, they noted improvements in lawns, flowers, driveways, shrubs, and the general appearance of the block and sent a note to the families concerned, congratulating them on making this improvement in the community. Some of the committees wrote to city officials when they noticed traffic hazards and hazardous or unclean conditions in streets or alleyways. They reported on the quality of the service they received in stores; when it was good, they wrote to the owners and expressed their appreciation. When a child reported a good experience with a policeman, a fireman, or a city employee, a letter of commendation would be sent to the central office. These are all ways of expressing one's concern and one's respect toward the community. Further, parents, teachers, and children are all working together in a common enterprise.

Bringing the Community Into the School

Still a third way of relating school and community concerns itself with bringing the community into the school. For example, are locally manufactured implements ever on exhibit in the school? Does the school display such manufactured objects in the main corridor and do they get moved from school to school so that teachers, students, and parents will have a chance to see them and take pride in them? If some things cannot be taken to the school, are there times when products are on exhibit elsewhere so that students and teachers can go to see them? Is any effort made through visits to stores, factories, libraries, laboratories, studios, or concert halls to discover things this community uses which have their origins in some foreign land? Are students learning something about the dependence of one community upon others?

Do citizens and visitors in the community visit the schools quite frequently? When we know that at almost any time interested people may drop into our school or classroom, it tends to make us just a little more alert, a little more interested in the relation between what we are doing and the community in which we live and work.

Components 5-6: Relating to the Outside World 57

What problems of the community and what data relating to the community are brought into the schools for study? Is there at least *one* copy of a local newspaper in every classroom? Are data presented which show the community's population growth according to the U. S. census? Do students have a chance to study how the community produces wealth and the changes that have taken place in this production over a period of years? Is there information on what happens to teen-agers who drop out of school? How many go to college and never come back to the community to live? Is this a financial loss to the community? How many people are unemployed, and for how long? What's wrong with the employment situation?

Are there some serious community problems which relate to segregation, and do these problems show up in churches, housing, industry, sports, or recreation and transportation? Is the community a "cultural desert," and if so, what can be done to make it a cultural oasis?

How many people move into and out of the community each year? A very high rate of turnover suggests low morale. When a child moves away from your community, what efforts are made to see to it that important social, intellectual, physical, and perhaps emotional data are shared with the staff of the distant school? When a new family moves into the community, what does the school and the individual classroom teacher do to make the orientation pleasant and effective?

Do students sometimes write to various foreign dignitaries to ask for information about their nations' schools and then compare their own education with that of French, German, or Russian children? Do they find out the size of classes in other lands, the texts used and how they are used, the homework assignments, the examinations, the kinds of punishments, and the kinds of rewards? And are they then asked to make some guesses about the communities which support those schools?

The Parent-Teacher Associations

There are some factors in the school-community relationships which perhaps can best be handled through preliminary discussions in the Parent-Teacher Association. If teen-age crime is indeed a community problem and if offenses against property and people are numerous, the PTA representatives would be most helpful in ascertaining the facts of the matter. They can and usually will go to the primary sources to get valid and reliable information. They often have inside information about children's fears, worries, and anxieties. They know their children's attitudes toward school. They generally know what their children do on the way to and from school, and they know quite well what their children do on weekends and during vacations. Knowing all of this, they have ideas about what their children need, and at PTA meetings they often advance these ideas in a sincere way.

The PTA meeting is the place—not to argue—but to listen and thank them for their suggestions. At these meetings the teacher should not complain about children, about the difficulties in teaching the underprivileged child, the slow child, and so forth. These are teaching problems; they do not concern the PTA in a public meeting. But the PTA is a place to take up the size of classes, the numbers of classes taught daily, the inadequacy of the buildings, equipment, or supplies. It is a place to talk about the need for the community to expand its programs for students in the arts and drama and music. It is a place to talk about values—and how there cannot be a community if people distrust each other and lie to each other; how there can be no community without respect for people and property. The PTA affords one the opportunity to talk about the relations of parents to children and of teachers to children, to join hands on many occasions and plan programs of working together, even to ask for the help of parents as teaching aides on some occasions. It is a place to ask questions about the costs of education and whether there are ways of eliminating the "hidden" costs that seem to accompany our ways of educating. It is a place to show one's respect for these parents who are sacrificing a great deal for their children and to make suggestions about extra services needed in the schools.

When teachers are carrying out the function of relating school to community, these meetings tend to be wholesome. Those who cooperate in a common endeavor tend to respect each other, tend to listen to each other, and on very many occasions want to help each other.

The School As a Public Exhibit

The fifth and final section pertaining to the component of school-community relationships reflects the desire of the community to use the school as a kind of public exhibit. The parents and the community generally look to the school for excellence in athletic competitions and performances. They want the school to put on musical events and school assemblies that reflect credit on the school and the community. They expect the school to organize and present dramatic productions. They want a "back to school" night, and sometimes they want exhibitions of artwork, academic work, or shop work. They want ceremonies

Components 5-6: Relating to the Outside World

at which honors and awards are bestowed and tasteful, well-organized graduation ceremonies. They want to see and hear good things about the local schools. They want our schools to prepare the students for college, and for those students not preparing for college they want other excellent programs.

In other words, in all of these public affairs, we are being judged as teachers. When we interact with the public at a PTA meeting, we are being judged in terms of our profession—teaching. When a child takes home a paper with our comments on it, the parent uses it as a basis for judging us as teachers. Whether we realize it or not, we as teachers are in the public arena.

One important component of teaching is an intelligent and persistent participation in the process of creating community-school relationships—not merely to have good relationships, although that may be important on special occasions. We want these relationships because we know that they are indeed the foundation of a better education for every child. If we are concerned about the quality of the community, and if the community becomes concerned about the quality of the schools, then both will tend to improve. All of the children, all of the teachers, and all of the community will benefit. This is *teaching*.

6

Components 7-8: Security Among One's Peers

COMPONENT 7: CREATING OPPORTUNITIES FOR EVERY STUDENT TO EARN STATUS AND RESPECT AMONG HIS PEERS

At the beginning of the year each person in a class, including the teacher, is a member—not of a group—but of an *aggregate*. One of the most difficult of all tasks in teaching is to succeed in developing a harmonious, working *group*. Most experienced teachers have memories of one or two wonderful groups; they also have memories of bad ones.

Speaking of the highly prized but rare and exceptional groups, the teacher is apt to say something like this: "I think I never did understand what made them so great as a group. They just seemed to click. I know that I was glad to come to school to work with them, and they seemed to come earlier and stay later. They accomplished so much, too. There were almost no discipline problems and the hours and the days and the weeks passed very quickly. They did so many different things. They published a weekly paper. They put on more than their share of assemblies. They collected old newspapers and sold them and were able to buy some equipment that they wanted. Nearly everyone had something to contribute to the group and the group seemed to appreciate it. They also had a pride in themselves as a group, and they would come to each other's defense. What's more, they all seemed to learn so much. Together, they worked like a *team*—they helped each other, cooperated with each other, praised each other, and at times sympathized with each other when one of them failed at something. Maybe I did something to help it along, but I can't pinpoint it. Maybe it was just a lucky combination of individual children. Whatever it was that brought it about, it surely was a wonderful experience for all of us. I'll remember them for many years to come."

A number of high school teachers have similar memories. A football coach will talk about a group that he remembers. He will say that the total squad did not have a large number of outstanding players but that, as a team, they clicked. They won a lot of games, but the important thing was the way they worked and played and laughed and cried—together! The teacher of dramatics will remember a year in which the dramatics group was "simply magnificent." The director of the band or chorus will also recall a year in which everything just seemed to flow together beautifully. The vocational teachers have told us of their joys in working with such groups. Practically every veteran teacher has had such an experience, and a number of them can recall a number of times when a group "clicked."

Of the many things which seem to characterize these harmonious groups, *two* are of great significance. In the first place they seem to have *power*—power to get things done, to influence one another, to withstand pressures, strains, and setbacks. Here we are talking about the type of power that is reflected in the unusual energies expended by members of the group, power that is disciplined by a sense of purpose and used in the best interests of the group and the individuals constituting the group. When referring to groups of this kind, teachers often say such things as: "They were a powerful group." "That team was a powerhouse." "They had powers that I never dreamed they had." In other words, a group that "clicks" is a group with power to do things.

In the second place such memorable groups seem to be characterized by unusually high *morale*. They seem to enjoy being together and working hard; they are flexible and can adapt to circumstances and to each other. There is an *esprit de corps*, a sense of loyalty to one's own inner self and to the group. They act naturally with each other; there is a calm and almost serene acceptance of themselves as a group and of each other as individuals. There is a positive valuation placed on themselves and on the group. Within the group each person seems to have some sense of personal worth: he not only belongs but he senses that he is valued. It is *not* a feeling of superiority; it is a feeling of security and assurance within the group. This is another of those many wonderful joys of living that money cannot buy and that happen by chance all too seldom.

Our many talks with experienced teachers have convinced us that the two factors, *power* and *morale*, are *always* associated with one another in the minds of the teachers. Does power produce morale of a high order? Is it the high morale that produces the power? Are there a number of factors, not yet mentioned, which tend to produce both power and morale almost simultaneously? We are pretty well convinced of the latter position. In cases where effective group power and high morale come into existence, we believe that the teacher *does* a number of things that facilitate their emergence.

We shall postpone for a short space all discussion of what the teacher *does* in favor of discussing the theory of power and morale which underlies this presentation. How do power and morale come into being within school groups? within the faculty as a group? within a community group? within any relatively small group that meets frequently?

Group Power in the Classroom

For most people *power* is a naughty word; there is something distasteful about it, even repugnant. Lord Acton's words have had wide circulation: "Power tends to corrupt and absolute power corrupts absolutely." Even in circumstances where people do indeed have power, they speak about it equivocally and suggest that in reality they have no power. There seems to be something a bit shameful in acknowledging that one has it. This general aversion to power may be related to a common misunderstanding of its meaning—that one has power when one can make another person do something that that person does not want to do. This suggests absolute control over another person, authority without limit, force, physical might, and perhaps even armed forces to produce acquiescence and obeisance. Here there is coercion or the threat of it to produce the desired action.

We see very little reason for accepting this meaning of power. We enter three objections:

1) One may grant that in the history of the race the concept of power as absolute authority was dominant for long periods.

The power was invested in an individual or a family and their actions could not be appealed. We submit that our age is greatly different from former times. We cannot compel an individual to take an occupation he does not want; we cannot force him to stay within the confines of a ghetto, town, or county. We cannot compel him to worship a certain God and do it in certain ways. Nor can we make him wear a certain garb, make him kneel, or kiss our hand or foot. Those days (we would like to think) are gone forever.

2) A second reason for rejecting the "I can force you" type of power is that power stops at that point when a person says *no*. And in recorded history there have been many instances in which individuals or groups have said *no*. In the very recent past, on more than fifty campuses, a number of students have said *no* and have brought collegiate and university processes to a stop. Classroom teachers are beginning to understand this limited scope of centralized power, but they are in the mood to say *no*. They want to share in decision making that not only affects their own lives but also affects the lives of the children they teach. When an individual or a group says *no*, that's where power stops: Organizations of Negroes have begun to say *no* and now demand a place in the power structure. The hard-core poverty groups are beginning to organize themselves in order to be able to say *no* to those who are exploiting them. We are not interested in the kind of power in which one person is trying to shove another person around.

3) In place of the "brute force" conception of power, we propose an alternative conception. We are interested in that kind of power that grows from within groups which meet face to face almost daily, if not more often. We are interested in that kind of power that is earned, not assigned, inherited, or maintained by might. This is the kind of power that is consistent with our democratic traditions.

With respect to *power*, some people believe that it resides within the individual person. Let us assume for the moment that the person is an elementary school principal. Over the past five years he has been the principal of a school that has developed a remarkably fine program. He has resigned and has accepted the position of principal at your school. Will he be a 'powerhouse' of a principal at your school? Will he bring his power with him and will he exert it in such a manner that almost surely your school too will develop a remarkable program? It is by no means a certainty that he will succeed again. He may fail in this new venture; the old program may stagger along as it is. We have only to study the history of executive staff changes to

Components 7-8: Security Among One's Peers

become fully aware of the fact that *power*—that is, *group power*—is not something that is carried around in one's pocket. Surely, that kind of power which we associate with high morale, joy in work, voluntary cooperation, *elan vital*, and *esprit de corps* is not the possession of an individual.

There are many people who believe that real power resides in the position, in the title. This is reflected in sayings like "If I were the principal of this school, I'd bring about a lot of changes." Maybe! If the power really did reside in the position, then *any* person in that position would be in the seat of power and would thus be a powerful person. He could indeed bring about a great many changes. Every principal would then have a faculty characterized by high morale which would be expending its energies cooperatively and effectively. However, we know that this just doesn't accord with reality. Evidently then, power neither resides in the person alone nor in the position itself.

Does power then reside in a constitution, in laws, perhaps in the rules and regulations of the institution? With respect to schools or departments of government, is it the red tape itself that is the source of power? Is power the one or several pieces of writing agreed to once upon a time and forever open to revision? In terms of the governance of the nation, the region, the state, or those very large aggregates of people who do not meet face to face, who have in effect a loose federation, who are seeking freedom and security for themselves and protection against possible tyrants, *power* is in individual men, in titles and positions and in written documents guaranteeing certain rights. Yet it is still more. If we are looking for participatory power, decentralized power, the power of groups to develop unique purposes and plans for their realization, the power to create new powers, the power to change with changing circumstances, we have to look for a different concept of power—one which is appropriate to the continuing functioning of people in groups who communicate with each other quite frequently.

Here, as we see it, are the basic notions of power in small groups, power of the kind we have been talking about:

1) In such groups, where every one is equal or thinks he is equal to everyone else, *there is no power in that group*—with respect to certain skills, qualities, or abilities—for the continuing achievement of power and morale.
2) A corollary of this first statement: In such groups power arises out of inequalities. The teacher does not wish for nor does he plan for homogeneity. Instead, he seeks op-

portunities for members of the group to distinguish themselves from one another—opportunities for them to earn status from their peers.

3) These inequalities have to be revealed to the members of the group. The group has to find out that these inequalities are present in their own group.

4) In such a group, when the inequalities have been revealed, they must also be accepted. In other words if the activity concerns marksmanship with a bow and arrow and if John proves himself to be the outstanding contender, his status as top man has to be acknowledged. The group must accept others, who prove themselves to be of average ability as having that status, and those who are lowest must be acknowledged as lowest.

5) Status within such a group is earned. It comes from revealing one's self in the group situation. Respect for one's status comes through being observed in action and in the group's verbal and nonverbal sharing of their reactions with each other. One or two members may not adequately estimate the status of a particular individual, or may not wish to accept it, but the public sharing of ten or twenty of one's peers is a most effective guard against this kind of prejudice.

6) A gradation of statuses tends to come into being. In many traits, skills, talents, and abilities, usually a very few stand out markedly as superior with respect to the rest of the group. Then there are a few more who are less talented, quite a few who are more or less average when compared to the group, and some who are markedly below this average. In other words, even within a very small group, a hierarchy tends to form.

7) This hierarchy is *a unit of power* within that group. It comes into being thru revealing, sharing, and accepting on a number of occasions.

8) As more and more such units of power accumulate within the group, that group develops high *morale*, and as the group uses this unit of power for its own purposes, it becomes a more powerful group.

According to all of this, if power is to develop, each individual within the group must get to know the others through the behavior which they exhibit in the group situation. One requirement, there-

Components 7-8: Security Among One's Peers

fore, of this teaching component is to create opportunities of various kinds for students to reveal themselves. As this process goes on, individuals get to know more about themselves. They also know the strengths and the weaknesses of the people with whom they are associating. They are learning how to discriminate the better from the worse and how to accept their own status and the statuses of their peers. They also learn to take pride in the accomplishments of any and nearly all the units of power that develop.

Developing Status

We now have to ask: Is *everything* to be revealed, or are there some guidelines to follow? Prof. Harold Lasswell and some of his associates at Yale University have written a volume entitled *Power and Personality* (2) in which they discuss eight factors which they believe to be important in the achievement of power. These are presented directly below, but not in order of importance and not in the same terms used by Lasswell.

1) *Skills that are prized by the group.* If baseball is prized by the group, those who are highly skilled in the game rise in the estimates of their fellows, and in this particular respect, rise in power. Where baseball is prized, a hierarchy will probably develop and a unit of power within the group has been created.

    Baseball is only one athletic skill. As opportunities are opened for a number of sports, different hierarchies will probably form and the group will take on added power in this large field. There are a great many possible skills from which to build units of power. There are the skills associated with excellence within each of the fields of the curriculum: arts, drama, and music; handicrafts; social skills; public speaking; weaving, sewing, and cooking; short story and poetry writing; as well as the skills of running meetings or managing projects, such as putting out newspapers and magazines. One part of the teacher's job is to find out what is likely to be prized; the second part is to create opportunities for students to participate and reveal themselves and thus earn status. The process is a step toward the creation of power and higher morale.

2) *Being well liked.* When one is high in the affection of his peers, it tends to give him some power in that group. He is wanted and liked and serves a cohesive function in the group. If one does not know anyone, there is little chance that he will be

liked. To achieve this kind of power, there must be opportunities to reveal those qualities which the group prizes. A hierarchy of "liked persons" develops and becomes a source of pride and power.

3) *Qualities associated with rectitude and conscience.* Where revealing takes place within a group, some individuals come to be known for their uprightness of character, for their strict honesty in human relationships. They seem to have a clear knowledge of right and wrong, have an inner compulsion to do what is right, and act "according to their conscience." People like this come to be respected and come to have some power within the group.

4) *Availability of resources.* The child who owns the bat and ball, the catcher's mitt, the mask, and the chest protector is very likely to be chosen as a member of the team. Some youngsters have money available for the purposes of the group, and these students often do not come from the wealthiest families. Some older children have a car at their disposal which can be made available for group purposes. Some young people make their homes available for a variety of purposes. This instant availability of resources for group purposes is often regarded as an asset that is prized, and those students with these assets come to have a certain power within the group.

5) *A sense of well-being and abundant health and energy.* No matter how busy they now are, some people are able to take on another task and yet another. They seem to have sources of energy that are inexhaustable, and they do the many chores of the group without excessive grumbling or complaining about their schedules. People with this energy, who are very willing to expend it in the interest of the group, come to have power in the group. They are prized by the group and are among the reasons for the high morale of the group.

6) *A wide range of information.* Those students who are unusually well informed about matters that interest the group rise in the esteem of the group. They come to have some power in that group. They are consulted when information is needed, and they are regarded as a valuable resource.

7) *Ability to influence and persuade.* In almost every group there are several people who seem to be able to charm others into accepting a course of action. Sometimes they use tactics that are close to threats and coercion. They speak with a verve, an enthusiasm, that sweeps you into agreement or acceptance. They too are sources of power within a group. Because they help to get assent and help to get things done, they have power and contribute to morale.

Components 7-8: Security Among One's Peers

8) *Respect for family class status.* Even amongst children there is an awareness of what is commonly called middle class values. The way children dress, the way they talk, they way they eat, their poise in social situations, the way they handle conflict—all point toward family background. Those with old family connections, those whose families have had money for generations, those who live in certain houses and have a certain style and status in the community have by virtue of that status a certain social power. When the social status of some students is higher than that of others, a certain deference is often shown to them. Since there is pride in having people like this in the group, they come to have some power in that group.

Let us assume that there is wide acceptance of these eight factors as sources of an individual's power as he interacts in group situations. Let us also assume that these factors are positive ones—not antisocial and hence not to be repressed. Let us also assume that they add zest to any person who is experiencing some increment of power as he earns status from his fellows, and that group morale does tend to improve.

It seems to us that when one accepts these ideas, one is also accepting the necessity for a component in teaching that provides opportunity for each student to earn status and respect from his peers. The idea of a rigidly narrow and severely restricted curriculum has to go by the board. The curriculum has to be opened up so that many different abilities and qualities may be revealed.

In many elementary school classrooms there is a rich curriculum. In others there is a solemn day-after-day preoccupation with the same textbooks and the same workbooks and with a never-ending emphasis upon reading, writing, and answering the teacher's questions. Quite obviously, with such a curriculum one can only excel in reading, writing, obedience, or clear speaking. Children with these qualities may do well, but in the classroom situation just described they are not likely to gain respect from their peers for having certain qualities. The curiculum is too restricted.

Many high school teachers say that within the confines of *their* subject matter, it is very difficult to think of ways of opening up the curriculum. But it can be done. If the topics are broad enough and if there are preliminary discussions about alternative topics, experiments, or people to be studied, students would then have a choice. When they have a choice, they are likely to choose something within their fields of interest and are more likely to excel and earn some status. Where they must always do what the teacher wants them to do, even if they do not like it, they will probably continue to earn low status and decrease morale.

This is especially true of students from a lower middle and lower social class backgrounds. In the homes of these families, as a general rule, there are very few books; reading is not highly prized, and book-learning as such, is something to be endured. Students from many of these families tend to perform poorly in reading, writing, and speaking 'correct' English. If they are required to reveal their *weaknesses* (not strengths) in reading and writing every day, if they get low grades for this achievement and little or no praise every single day, and if over and over again they get too few chances to succeed, to feel a sense of power, and to earn the respect of their peers, you can be sure that their morale will go down. You can also be sure that a power base is not being built.

In addition, when students have little opportunity to succeed, they tend to get into trouble. The teacher who does not provide success opportunities for these youngsters is creating behavior problems, perhaps without realizing it. These children can *think* as well as other children. They can compare things and see likenesses and differences. They can report their observations. Their attitudes and opinions, hopes and aspirations, feelings, cares, and worries are all waiting to be revealed. They have beliefs and convictions about the world in which we live and in a situation in which their feelings are respected, they are willing to share these beliefs and convictions.

Such children can socialize just as well as any other child can. Many are extremely clever with their hands and can earn status by performing tasks that require dexterity. They can and often do excel in sports and games. And as nearly all veteran teachers know, they are often extremely sensitive to being treated unfairly. Some research evidence indicates that they are the ones who are most frequently bawled out before the entire class. They are the students who out of all proportion to their numbers get the lowest grades.

Because these students tend to be poor in reading, teachers in some schools emphasize reading all day long. Just imagine what this experience must be like if one does not do so well in that activity. If school experiences are rich and varied, there is a much better chance that the student will like education. The wise teacher will emphasize the relation of school and community and the processes of thinking and valuing. If the teacher is often *showing how* and thus imparting skills of various kinds, if materials within the student's scope of experience *supplement* the texts and workbooks, and if the teacher pays attention to the needs of each child, then school becomes an inviting, engaging, and often exciting experience.

Components 7-8: Security Among One's Peers

We are appropriately proud of our country and of its traditions which emphasize *equal opportunity for all*, especially in the area of education. But just saying so doesn't make it so. We must see to it that opportunities for *all* are indeed provided. If we have a school and a curriculum that provides opportunities mainly for white middle class children, we are not being faithful to our democratic traditions. We must see to it that these opportunities are extended to all colors and creeds, to both rich and poor and to those in between. When we create opportunities for *every* student to earn status and respect among his peers, we are carrying out that pledge.

Helping Students Earn Status and Respect

In order to carry out this component of teaching, the teacher will need to pay a lot of attention to individual differences. As a general rule, he will not give the same assignment to everyone in the class. Students will be studying from different texts, and the work will be adapted more to the individual needs of the students because they will have a choice in what they are to study.

Teachers will also get to know much more than they do now about the out-of-school interests of their students. At the high school level more teachers will be going to athletic events and school events of all kinds. Through this attendance they will begin to learn about the high status of a great many of their students. High school teachers will read the school newspaper much more regularly and carefully to see what it says about individuals who are a part of the student body.

In any class—whether science, art, math, literature, shop, or foreign language—a short time could be set aside each week for a brief discussion of the extracurricular events of the past week. This is almost the only way that teachers have of identifying with the student body, of communicating to students their pride and concern for the activities of school life. School life becomes community life when *both* students and faculty participate. If teachers appear only in classrooms, they will be missing important opportunities to learn how specific students relate to their peers. If they do not open ways for earning a variety of statuses, much of the power within their classes will lie dormant and morale will wane.

What do teachers do who carry out this teaching component? (1) They are sensitive to the need for a rich variety of experiences. (2) They design a number of special assignments for individual children so that these children might earn status and respect. (3) They reach outside the classroom to find out about their own students. Teachers who are fulfilling this component discover the status of students among their peers by attending school events, by reading about them, and by talking with other students about them from time to time. (4) They find opportunities to praise students for school achievements. Teachers *don't* tell students, "Some day you will be somebody." They help these children to be somebody right now.

In research carried out at New York University (5) there was substantial evidence to the effect that classes in which teachers know what students think of each other have higher morale. In other related research it was found that in classes where morale is high, the teacher's judgments of students meriting praise is positively correlated with the students' own judgments.

Much has been said about power and morale, about those personality factors which Lasswell (2) cites as important for earning status and creating opportunities for children to reveal themselves to one another. Not very much has been said about poor morale. How does it show itself? A great deal of absences and tardiness may be a symptom of low morale. If the students divide into cliques or gangs, if they have almost nothing to do with each other after school and during weekends, if they "run down" the group, then one can be fairly sure that morale is low. If their achievement is poor and they don't care, or if they have a thousand and one excuses for doing little, this too is a sign that morale is not what it should be. Bickering, squabbling, fighting, and public criticism of each other—much of it crude and bitter—all mean that something is wrong.

If you, as a teacher, sense that you do not respect the group, if every night when you go home you are completely tired out, and if you drag your feet in the morning and are somewhat disinclined to show up for teaching, you can be quite sure that your class is not a powerful group. You can also be reasonably sure that classroom morale is poor. If you find yourself saying such things as "You have to watch them every minute," or "You just can't trust them out of your sight," then you will know that both power and morale are missing. There is little unified purpose and almost no cooperation within such a group.

If you are creating opportunities for every child to earn status and respect from his classmates, you will be helping to bring power and high morale into being. This provision for individual differences, this opportunity for each child to help choose what he wants to study, this wide and rich curriculum which you offer, along with your in-

Components 7-8: Security Among One's Peers

terest in the extracurricular life of your students and your acknowledgment of their achievements in many fields outside of class, are all indications of meeting the requirements of this seventh component—helping students to earn status.

COMPONENT 8: CREATING EMOTIONAL SECURITY IN THE LEARNING SITUATION

This vital component of teaching puts a great emphasis upon the *feelings* of children, particularly their feelings of emotional security, which are so important to the learning process. First, what are some of the more general factors which contribute to feelings of security? (1) *The teacher's behavior must be highly consistent.* Students have to be able to predict it and depend on it. They must be relatively *sure* of it. You can't be widely permissive one moment and severely restrictive the next; nor can you be gentle, warm, and accepting one moment and just the opposite a few minutes later. If you are highly *in*consistent, students will not know how to relate themselves to you; they will be insecure, and instead of relaxing as they work and study, they will be keeping one eye and one ear open. No two of us teach exactly alike; our patterns of behavior differ. Each of us however has an obligation to be consistent within our pattern when we work with a group.

(2) *Children need to know the limits of acceptable behavior.* The teacher must let them know that there are rules and that he will hold them to the rules. There are, of course, exceptions for most unusual circumstances, but these exceptions cannot be examples of favoritism for one or a few children. It is a good idea to work these rules out with the group in the earliest meeting days and to put them in a prominent place on the blackboard or bulletin board. Children feel more secure when they know for sure what is acceptable and what is not acceptable. Note: It is not wise to have too many rules.

(3) *Students need to feel physically secure.* They ought to feel that the teacher is their defender in all times of trouble, discomfort, or danger. Even when they are fighting with each other, children on many occasions actually *want* the teacher to stop the fight. If a child has an accident of some kind, he wants the teacher's help and sympathy. If a child is threatened by another child, who may be older and bigger, he wants the teacher to intercede. If a child is not feeling

well, he wants the teacher to be concerned about him. A teacher who comes to the defense of an individual child or an entire group is providing emotional security.

(4) *Every student feels more secure if he knows that the teacher will not diminish his status in the presence of his peers.* This means that practically *all* punishments will be administered privately. No child should receive the scorn, ridicule, sarcasm, or name-calling of an angry or upset teacher in a group situation.

(5) *Students want a teacher who can save them from extremes of humiliation.* Nearly all of us have learned a great deal through the mistakes we have made. Sometimes, however, a mistake made in the presence of our peers can be terribly humiliating. Sometimes a teacher can very quickly assert that he himself is partly to blame for the situation. Sometimes he can restate what a student has said in a manner that robs it of its adverse effect. Sometimes he can turn it into a joke on himself. Whatever he does, he tried to soften the significance of the mistake in order to help the student "save face."

(6) *Students feel more secure when the teacher is relaxed and pleasant.* They like to be welcomed in the morning and they like to have someone say good night after the last class of the day. Some teachers make it a point to shake hands with each child at the close of the school day. Others make it a point to wish them happy weekends when Friday comes to an end. Many teachers have a sense of humor and share a joke or a funny story with their class.

(7) *Students feel more secure when the teacher's explanations, directions, and comments are clear and to the point.* If the teacher leaves them confused, the students feel insecure. Students have to feel free to ask questions, to say when they do not understand, and to expect a courteous response from the teacher.

(8) *Students feel more secure when they are with a teacher whom they consider to be fair.* "Fair" is a word that children often use when they make comments about their teachers. It may be fair to have a rule that all children must take off their hats when they are in the class room, but it would *not* be fair to require all children to wear hats of the same size. We may require all children to work, but it is unfair on many occasions to require that they do exactly identical work. Assignments, tests, and examinations should be fair; punishments and praise as well as grades and awards should be fair. A teacher who is *fair* adds to the emotional security of the learning situation.

(9) *Students feel more emotionally secure when they are respected.* This means that the teacher *listens* to them and responds to them. At times he will ask for their help, their ideas, and their opinions. He will

avoid the repeated use of such statements as "You're too young," "You're too small," or "You wouldn't understand." The teacher doesn't "run down" the group, the school, or the grade level. Instead, he takes many opportunities to acknowledge the achievements of the school and the group.

(10) *Students feel more secure where there is a relative absence of fear.* Where the teacher's pattern of behavior includes threats, warnings, or shouting, or where the teacher is often suspicious of the students or sets traps in order to catch them doing something amiss, children can feel the tension in the air. Learning suffers because their emotional security is threatened.

(11) *Students feel much more secure when they believe that their teacher is loyal to them.* This means that the teacher keeps his promises and takes such promises seriously. It means that he will not gossip about them to other teachers and that he will not tell other students what has been told to him in confidence. It means that he will believe what the children say until there is real evidence which is contradictory.

(12) *Students feel more secure when school becomes a place where they can "live", not a place where they must serve time.* Many kinds of behavior should be permitted so long as they do not interfere with the purposes of learning. Students want the freedom to stretch their legs once in a while or to talk quietly with their peers—sometimes to "do nothing", to be free from pressure for a few minutes.

To feel emotionally secure in the learning situation students need to feel wanted and liked. That is, they need some warmth and affection if they are to learn. They need to feel that they really *belong* to the group, that they are missed by the group when they are absent. They feel like rejects when they are sent out into the hall, into the cloakroom, or to the principal's office. They need to have their feelings of fear and guilt diminished and their feelings of achievement and accomplishment strengthened. They need a teacher who will listen and respond, one who is patient with their endless questions, one who is helping them to understand themselves and the world in which they live.

The teacher who tends to be guided by the *do's* and *don'ts* outlined in this section is providing emotional security for children. He is supplying a secure environment in which learning can take place. Moreover, what he does in this respect is observable: he will be *teaching*.

7

Components 9-10: Helping Students to Learn and Grow

COMPONENT 9: DIAGNOSING AND REMEDYING LEARNING DIFFICULTIES

Some people think that those who practice a profession have "the answers" to the problems in their field. Such professionals do have some of the answers, but on many occasions they are baffled by the specific situation confronting them. The practicing doctor does not always *know* what is wrong with his patient. After he has studied the data and examined the patient, he often seeks additional information, sometimes the advice of colleagues or specialists of one kind or another. He formulates a "hunch"—the best guess in that particular situation. Basing his diagnosis on that hunch, he suggests a program of treatment. If that program does not seem to work, the hunch is discarded and another one is formulated and tried.

In every professional field the practitioners face problems of various degrees of difficulty. It is a natural and accepted part of their work. The opthalmologist meets with conditions of the eye which he does not immediately understand. The engineer very frequently has to face up to new and unusual technical difficulties. The lawyer sometimes has a case that represents a very involved legal problem. If people did not have problems, we probably would not have the professions.

So it is with teachers. They frequently encounter learning problems. It is an inescapable part of their profession. Moreover, they are expected to have hunches about what the difficulties are in a particular case. They are supposed to know the common causes of learning difficulties, to make a "best guess" in the case of a particular student, and to work with that student in ways that are consistent with that hypothesis. When they are completely baffled, or when they think that the needed treatment should come from a specialist, they are expected to make a report to that effect.

At this particular moment in time, our profession is in a very difficult position. There are so many things about learning that we do not fully understand. We need the help of many disciplines and many different kinds of professionals if we are to find a secure base for our hunches. Fortunately, we are beginning to get this kind of help. Neurologists, psychologists, and physiologists have studied memory processes and other activities of the brain. Sociologists, anthropologists, and economists have entered our domain and are working on some of the very involved problems in the area of learning. New kinds of regional educational research centers are being organized to tackle some of our more baffling problems. New technologies are also entering our field which will probably contribute greatly to our effectiveness in the areas of drill and recall and the general communicating of information. This help will be greatly appreciated.

We teachers need to become familiar with the newer media: videocorders, tape recorders, learning machines, and devices of many kinds, including those which focus upon reading as a skill. We need to free ourselves from the many routine tasks so that we can take the time to emphasize thinking, values, community relations, as well as emotional security and the achievement of status and respect. We must have the time to study individual children and modify the curriculum in their interest, diagnose their learning difficulties, and formulate hunches to guide us in working with them.

In terms of our present knowledge, what can we do when we are confronted with a student who seems to be having learning difficulties?

Health Defects

Difficulties in learning may result from deficiencies in the student's health. We do not diagnose what is wrong in this area, but in practically every case where there is some difficulty in learning we should

Components 9-10: Helping Students to Learn and Grow

raise the question: Is it likely to be related to the student's health? Behavior problems often have their roots in health defects. Reading difficulties are often explained by factors affecting vision. Effective note-taking on the part of students often depends upon their having normal hearing.

Most of us are acutely sensitive to some of the very obvious signs that something is wrong with a student's health: blotches on the skin; frequent requests to leave the room; extreme and unusual floridity of countenance or unusual pallor; an emaciated, tired appearance; a face contorted with pain; a limp that appears suddenly; a kind of languor and passivity that is unusual for a particular student; or a persistent hacking cough. A student who quite frequently falls asleep at his desk or one who tells you openly that he has a stomach ache, headache, toothache, or earache must be cared for appropriately. These things come to our attention in rather direct ways.

From our own experiences with illness, most of us know how difficult it is to become interested in the learning of new concepts, the development of a new skill, and the maintenance of excellent human relationships with our family and friends *when we are ill*. As a matter of fact, when we are not acting like our usual self, a close family member is quite apt to ask: "Are you feeling all right?" If this is true of those we know best, why should we not have the same kind of hunch about the students whom we teach? We suggest that in almost every case the teacher should respond to his *first hunch* that something is wrong. We should try to find out from the nurse, from the child himself, or from his parents if everything is satisfactory from the standpoint of the child's physical health. We should not say positively that there is something wrong and we should not make any attempt to label the situation. That is the work of a medical doctor. We should, however, be sensitive to the role that good health plays in the learning process, and when something is going wrong with normal learning, we should *first of all* suspect that it might very well be poor health. We might suggest, in many cases, that the student undergo a rigorous physical examination.

During the past decade in particular, we have found that many students have heart trouble of many kinds and even ulcers. We know that there are a number of child suicides each year. There are good sound reasons for suspecting poor health when learning problems become more acute. Until this hunch or hypothesis is deemed to be irrelevant, we should not formulate a substitute for it. Pay attention *first of all* to the child's physical health as a possible cause of learning difficulty.

Study Skills and Work Habits

We are going to assume that every teacher can and does make the ordinary investigation of possible shortcomings in *study skills and work habits*. Does the student have the prerequisites for doing the work you have assigned him or that he has chosen to do? Can he and does he read at the required grade level? Does he know how to get the meaning of a paragraph or story? Does he know how to use a book, its table of contents, and its index? Does he know how to study? Does he know some of the important principles for effective study? What are his habits with respect to studying? Does he know how to make notes that recall his studying? Are the notes useful in summarizing his work? Teachers must make a search into the student's academic background to see if he has a sound basis for the work that is at hand. On many occasions a student simply needs some focused, remedial work before he is ready to go ahead. This is true not only of reading; it is also true of practically every skill and subject matter area.

Emotional Disturbances in Normal Children

Let us assume that we have checked off physical health as a probable explanation and that we find nothing wrong with the student's study skills and work habits. What might be another plausible line of investigation which may assist a student with learning difficulties? It would depend, of course, upon your observations of the specific student. If you suspect that something is wrong with his feelings of emotional security, the youngster is probably behaving in one or more of the following five patterns:

1) He is unusually *aggressive* in his relations with his peers and often with his teacher and frequently *hostile* and sometimes *violent* in his reactions to others. He may be very loud in his name-calling of others or get into fights with his peers. His aggression might also be directed toward property; he might deface or destroy books, mark up his desk, turn on faucets and plug up sinks, or "lose" property that is quite valuable. He seems to do all of these things too often, and he does them with seemingly slight provocation. When this kind of behavior shows up, the problem is likely to be frustration: his deep-seated emotional needs are *not* being met. If this is a reasonable hunch or hypothesis for the particular child, then as we expend efforts to meet those needs, his behavior should change. More will be said about this later.

Components 9-10: Helping Students to Learn and Grow

2) He is unusually *shy, reticent,* or *withdrawn* in his behavior. He is a loner; he isn't *in* the class—he is on the outside looking in. He manages his life in such a way that he seldom has much to do with any of his classmates. This kind of withdrawal from the world suggests that some emotional needs have not been met. As we try to meet those needs and if our hypothesis is sound, he will change his behavior. He will increase his group participation and will increase the frequency and warmth of his human contact. (We must remember, too, that some individuals are supremely happy in the company of themselves; they really do not need involvement with other humans of their age and grade level.) In cases where our hypothesis or hunch is refuted, we must try another.

3) Some children with emotional problems may be neither aggressive nor withdrawn. They may reveal their insecurities by *regressive behavior.* If you are teaching sixteen-year-olds, one of them might begin acting like a ten-year-old. If you are teaching six-year olds, one of them might begin acting like a babe-in-arms. This regression to an earlier stage of behavior is often connected with unfulfilled emotional needs. In other words, it is a good hunch to suspect that the regressing child is experiencing what are for him rather severe emotional stresses and strains.

4) Emotional stress sometimes shows itself in *submissive behavior* —fawning, toadying, yielding to others, acting as if one does not have a backbone. Such a child seldom if ever dissents or protests but may cry easily and often. A child who persistently behaves in such a manner is often used as a scapegoat by the class. It is a fairly good hunch that this kind of child is experiencing emotional difficulties.

5) Indications of *psychosomatic disturbances* are frequently associated with emotional strains of one kind or another. Symptoms of physical illness tend to appear when the child is working under some stress or worry. He may have these symptoms when he has to read, when he has to work with mathematics, or during recess, art, or shop. The evidence: He may reveal his problem with headaches, stomach aches, minor skin eruptions, toilet troubles, or more serious outbursts of asthma or hayfever, or palpitations. Look for a pattern when these symptoms appear.

Persistent patterns of *aggression, withdrawing, regression, submissiveness,* or *psychosomatic disturbance* are all indications of possible emotional strain. Where one or several of these syndromes is observed, the teacher's next step is to study the child for a few days to get some inkling of his unmet emotional needs. Methods for doing this and suggestions for ways a teacher might help such children are contained in "The Problem Child" (7).

Thinking-Related Behavior

Over and over again in their written and oral reports of individual children teachers indicate a relationship between the behavior of a child and inadequacies of thinking:

1) *Impulsive.* Teachers say such things as "He doesn't stop to think. He goes off half-cocked, or acts thoughtlessly."
2) *Too dependent.* Here again the comments are related to thinking. Teachers say that the student does not do his own thinking, that he depends upon others to do his thinking for him.
3) *Misses the meaning.* Teachers say that the student "doesn't seem to understand," "doesn't get the point," or "doesn't think very well."
4) *Can't concentrate.* Teachers say that he "doesn't keep his mind on his work." "He's a scatterbrain—his mind drifts off in all directions." "If he would only think about what he is doing, he would be all right."
5) *Has all the answers; a loud mouth.* He thinks that if he outshouts the others, he has won the argument. He is deadsure, positive about so many things and unable to hear what the others are saying.
6) *The one-track mind.* Teachers say that he becomes confused if one tries to show him a second or third alternative. He would like to believe that there is *only one way* to do most anything. He is rigid, inflexible, and not adaptable in problematic situations.
7) *Afraid to think.* Teachers say of these students that they *lack confidence in their ability to think.* They seldom offer suggestions in a group situation; they come around later and talk about what they "wanted to say." They need more experiences which involve thinking.
8) *The rote learner.* Teachers say of these children that they "don't want to be required to think." They want to read, remember, and say back. They don't like situations where they have to think.

In all of these cases we suggest that the remedies lie in a curriculum that emphasizes thinking, and the patient, informed, helpful behavior of the teacher. We believe that the curriculum should stress these operations:

a) Observing
b) Comparing
c) Summarizing
d) Classifying
e) Interpreting
f) Problem solving
g) Criticizing
h) Imagining
i) Decision making
j) Looking for assumptions
k) Working on larger projects
l) Hypothesizing

In addition, we believe that in listening to students and in reading their papers, teachers should be alert to the possible coding of extreme expressions, to the use of either-or arguments and unsupported if-then generalizations, to the use of similes and metaphors, to value judgments of many kinds, and to attributions made about the behavior of others. Three colleagues and I have written at length about these matters in *Teaching for Thinking* (8). The reader will find in that book many suggestions and examples of each of the operations listed above. The book also contains references to the research which supports these approaches to an emphasis on thinking and the changes which take place in the behavior of children when such emphases are made.

Value-Related Behavior

We think of values as giving direction to life. They represent something that we prize and cherish; they represent our own personal choices, our preferences. Moreover, before choosing them, we thought about them, thought about alternatives, and anticipated the consequences of our choices. That is, we knew what we were doing. The choice we made was not an isolated choice, not a single-shot experience: what we value we are very likely to choose again and again, varying our behavior somewhat in varying circumstances. We are likely to expend money to fulfill the value, to pledge time to it, to share it with friends. We would probably read about it and talk about it, and in many ways it would influence our style of living. That is, because we live it, we would defend it.

Values grow out of our life experiences, and as we broaden and deepen our experiences, we reconstruct our values. That is to say, as we broaden ourselves, we are valuing. To be alert and alive to the values in a situation, to be free to choose, and to choose freely after due consideration is to give direction to one's life. It also adds to the zest of living. What are some of the characteristic ways of living and behaving which indicate the absence of values on the part of an individual?

1) *Apathy, indifference.* There seems to be an absence of any controlling purposes, a lack of interest and concerns, few signs of aspiration, and no strongly organized attitudes or beliefs. The student displays no strong feelings about school activities, either academic or extracurricular, and seems almost alienated. We suggest that he needs help in developing values. We have already written something about ways of doing this when we discussed this teaching component in Chapter 5 (Component 5). We suggest again that teachers might find it very profitable to consult the volume *Values and Teaching* (9).

2) *Flightiness of behavior.* Here we have the student who is interested in almost everything but only for a very short time. He flits from one thing to another and seldom settles down for serious work, play, or study. Teachers quickly recognize the absence of organized and serious purposes and interests. The problem here again is to help the youngster develop values.

3) *Overconformity to the teacher.* If one does not have values of one's own (or a life of one's own), one is quite likely to live the life of some other person and to adopt his values. There are students in our schools who want to live the teacher's life. They study the teacher's facial expressions and gestures and pay particular attention to the words he uses and his intonations. They are trying to find out what the teacher wants, and then they try to give it to him. Because they lack purposes, concerns, and convictions of their own, they will borrow them temporarily from the teacher. As they meet another teacher, they will borrow from him, and this process goes on and on. These students need help in the development of values.

4) *Overdissenters.* Again and again, these students complain, whine, or persistently ask questions about the curriculum, the rules and regulations, the books, the activities, and just about everything. They do this in a carping, protesting manner. Teachers say of such children, "I know a hundred things he is against, but I don't know one thing that he is *for*." Unfortunate but true: he isn't *for* much of anything. Purposes do not seem

to be there; serious interests and concerns are not present. What he and others like him need is a great deal of help in the development of values.

5) *Pretenders, role players.* We sometimes meet students who vividly reenact a character that they have seen on TV or one whom they have read about. If a teacher leaves the classroom, one of these students is apt to imitate him before the class. These students wear many hats and seem to have no hat of their own; they tell stories about themselves which stretch the truth quite a good bit. Not having a self (purposes, goals, interests, concerns), they make up a self, and then another one. They are not only in trouble but they know that something is wrong. They need and want help in developing a self and developing values. As in the other categories, we are speaking only of extreme cases of such behavior.

6) *Very inconsistent attitudes.* This is the student who expresses a very extreme attitude one day, and a few days later he expresses the very opposite extreme. He likes something one day and detests it on another. Teachers say of such a child, "He's a very confused person—he seems to be all mixed up." He is confused, but telling him that he is confused doesn't help much. He needs help in developing those values which will give direction to his life.

7) *Can't make up his mind.* Suppose that there is very little in life that you prize or cherish; it would then be difficult for you to make up your mind. In the absence of values, most everything appears to be a dull gray in color. Nothing appeals, nothing entices, nothing leads one to choose. In choice situations one is very uncertain; it is hard to make a choice. He doesn't know how to choose; he has no touchstone with which to measure the alternatives before him. Such students need much help, and they need it daily if they are to develop a strong set of values.

8) *Cynics who are often underachievers.* Some students are suspicious of the value of everything. Nothing matters very much to them except their own personal feelings of insecurity. They seem to have given up the hope that it is worthwhile to have purposes, aspirations, and concerns. Often they do not put forth much effort. Teachers say, "They could do much better but they don't try very hard." Like any of us, they need direction, a purpose they can prize, and zestful ways of channeling their energies, but they don't seem to be equal to the task. They need the help of an informed, insightful teacher who will listen and interact and help them to find themselves.

We shall return to the headings of these categories in the next section, which deals with evaluating, recording, and reporting. Before we close this section, however, let us repeat a few things. Several times we have said that values grow out of our life experiences and our reflections upon them. We have mentioned several times that the quality of our life experiences is of tremendous importance in our growth and development. We quoted a short passage by John Dewey on the importance of ideal school experiences. We have stressed the importance of a curriculum that puts an emphasis upon thinking, values and valuing, and the relationships of schools and their communities. We have indicated the great need for continuous modification and supplementation of the curriculum to make it alive and vibrant with experience.

When teachers inform and explain, when they show how, they can —if they choose—deal with trivia. If the broad outlines of the curriculum emphasize the great ideas of all time and tie them in with the local community and personal living, this makes all operations doubly significant. Valuing and value development take place against a background of experience. What is the quality of that experience? Should *every* institution, including the schools and especially your own school, be judged according to the experiences which you now offer to children and which are shaping the future of these children and their world? Are you proud of what the schools now offer as a way of living for children? Do you cherish it? If there were other alternatives, including one you might suggest, would you nevertheless choose the pattern that now operates in your school? Do you stand up and defend it? Do you make sacrifices to further its purposes? If you do, you value what is going on now and you will help to perpetuate it.

Morale and Power

In Chapter 6 the teaching component dealing with classroom morale and power (Component 7) was discussed at some length. There we argued that in order to earn status and respect from one's peers, one had to *do* something in the presence of those peers; one had to reveal one's self. This means that the members of the group have to get to know each other, and in a great variety of ways. The curriculum must be rich, varied, and flexible. The student's out-of-school interests and activities have to be represented. The emphasis is upon *earning respect and status—earning* it from those with whom one lives day in and day out.

Components 9-10: Helping Students to Learn and Grow

Many of the signs of poor morale were listed in that section. So far as the classroom is concerned, paying attention to these signs will provide a sensitive, inquiring teacher with practically all the evidence he needs about the quality of morale in the room. Using these criteria, he cannot say anything as absurd as "In my room the morale is 74.29." Who cares? Is it reasonably good? Is it bad to very bad? What are some of the negative symptoms, if any? Does the group show pleasure in being at school? Are they glad to come, and do they look forward to tomorrow? Are they vitally engaged in work that interests them? Do they look out for each other and protect each other, and are they proud of the group? Many other questions were suggested or implied in the previous discussion of this topic.

In her research dealing with power in classroom groups, Prof. Lucy Polansky of Queens College developed some sociometric tests based upon Lasswell's categories. These were extremely useful in her research, which required several estimates of the status of each individual child. But for the morale of the group, such individual testing is unnecessary. It is the *morale of the group* that is highly related to the *power of the group*. The criteria for diagnosing morale will give a teacher a good sense of the morale status of the group of children with whom she is living and working.

In addition to what he sees and hears within the room, the teacher may find supplementary evidence from other sources. If one's relationships with these other sources are good, the evidence tends to come without the asking. Mothers and fathers say things that very often are related to morale. Other teachers say things that they have picked up from other sources. The principal very often gets word of outstanding interest or disgust for groups in his school. The staff which represents special services—the school nurse, the school psychologist, the guidance department, the social service people, and the people in the arts, crafts, and music—have information to share. Teachers who play a prominent role in extracurricular activities pick up much information about the quality of morale. If one is concerned about it, if one values it, then one can learn to make a rough estimate of the situation.

COMPONENT 10: RECORDING AND REPORTING

Recording something is nearly always the first step toward reporting something. A communications system begins to take shape. There are times when the teacher records information intended only for himself at that moment. With the accumulation of more such records and with data from other sources, he feels that he is on solider ground in preparing the report. Without certain kinds of records, he cannot make certain kinds of reports. If we study a teacher's reports very carefully, we can infer with some reliability what it is that he keeps track of. And conversely, if we know what he is doing *when he is teaching*, we would normally expect that his reports would grow out of what he prizes with respect to *education and teaching*.

But the teacher may encounter difficulties with the administration. They (the anonymous *they*) may insist upon complete and prompt absence and tardiness reports and the ubiquitous "grade cards." "They" may not want anything else. Be patient about all of this. We are going to say something about administrators in the closing chapter of this book.

(1) *Grade cards.* Most of the teachers we have talked with believe there is a real need for this type of reporting, but they would like to see some modification of the existing practice. Recognizing the large amount of money and time now expended on standardized tests, these teachers suggest that (*a*) in October of every school year the parents should receive a record of the child's accomplishments according to these tests of achievement. The card should contain suggestions for reading and interpreting the information. (*b*) Then in late May, after the tests have been administered a second time, the results should again be reported to the parents. The parents would then have information about their child's growth or lack of it in reading speed and comprehension, spelling, mathematics, language usage, and social studies. If the local administration and teachers accept this as one method of evaluating the work of students, then the results should be shared with the parents, who are after all vitally interested in the matter.

(2) *Written reports to parents.* Many teachers agree with the idea that the reports should reflect at least a few of the major components of teaching as expressed in the preceding pages. For example, parents should be informed about the content of the education that has gone on during the period of a month. What has the class studied? What has the class talked about at some length? What has been explained to the children? What "showing how" of a major and difficult skill has been emphasized? What kinds of relationships has the group had with the community? Were there visits to the community? Were community members in the classroom as speakers, consultants, helpers, or observers? What use has been made of audiovisual aids and the various teaching and learning machines now available?

If a teacher keeps a diary of what is going on, all of these records would be available for the writing of a monthly summary, which would then be mimeographed. As children get older and get some command of writing, each would write out what *he* did in the context of the group's work. This would be attached to the mimeographed sheet along with samples of the written work of each child. The parent, under these circumstances, begins to know what is going on in school, since the school is taking the responsibility of informing them.

(3) *Oral reports to parents.* This is one of the best opportunities to relate school and community. It is most successful when parents and teachers are talking together about the life of the child, his strengths and his weaknesses. It is a private discussion; there is nothing in writing for the parent to take home.

What should the focus of the discussion be? We suggest that the diagnostic categories should be a primary concern of the teacher. Does the student seem to be emotionally secure, are his needs reasonably well met, or is he showing symptoms of aggression, of withdrawal, regression, submission, or psychosomatic illness? Does he appear to be well physically, or should some questions be raised about this vital matter with the parents? How does he get along with his peers? In what ways has he earned status and respect among them? What about his thinking operations—is he fairly normal, or does he fall rather clearly into one of those diagnostic categories? What does he seem to prize and cherish? Does he have purposes and does he work at them? What interests has he displayed? If a teacher is able to talk to a mother and father about their child in terms of these categories, the parents will know that the school is concerned about some very important educational matters. Parents also become more interested in these same matters when they know that school and community are uniting in a common task.

The first such meeting cannot be unduly negative. Where the picture does indeed seem black, the teacher may have to *search* for items that have some positive value. In almost every instance this is not difficult.

We suggest that the interview conclude with a discussion of the experiences that the student is having both within the school and outside, that is, at home. What things does he do that are a bit out of the ordinary: travel, museums and art galleries, movies and plays, or camping away from home over night? What does he look at on TV and how much time does he usually spend on it? Does he have any hobbies or interests that the school should know about? Are the parents reasonably happy with the friends that the child has, or does he need more and different ones? What responsibilities does he have at home, and does he discharge them rather faithfully? What is he reading? In what ways can the school do more to help in his development? In all of these ways you are getting across the idea that the highest quality of experience, in school and out of school, is not too good for their child. You are saying that the best possible experiences are within reach and that with intelligent planning their child can share in them. This is one way of trying to unite the school and the community, giving both a common purpose and a shared responsibility.

(4) *Reporting to students.* When we return a written paper or some other product to a student with our *written* comments on it, we are, perhaps without realizing it, reporting to him. Whatever we report tends to be taken as important because we are the teachers. In many instances, the student takes the materials home and shares them with his family. Our comments are now on parade. Did we notice *only* the shortcomings in the work, or did we recognize and comment upon some of its *positive* aspects? Did we say something significant, something helpful, something that might lead to further reflection? Did we make a number of judgments about the student, or did our comments refer to his *work*? Did we call *values and thinking* to his attention? We always need to remember that when we are reporting, we are teaching, and our teaching stands revealed.

Sometimes we report *orally* to a student, and we do it privately. We may be raising questions about his behavior in class; we may be telling him of some emphasis he needs to make in his approach to studying. We may say many positive things in this private, oral report, and if we have negative things to say, we almost never say them unless in private. This too is teaching, and it is recognized as such by the student.

In reporting to students, we sometimes do it in front of the whole class. There are times when our report concerns the whole class— their achievements, their strengths and weaknesses as revealed on a test or on an assignment that has been handed in, or their general behavior in the school, the corridors, and the classroom. On some occasions we make personal references to individual students. This is a delicate matter, both with praise and censure. When you do this, the child and his status are under the scrutiny of the entire group. What you say may be as important for you as for him. If he has indeed earned a high status with his peers and your remarks tend to undercut that status, you may lose status as a result. Public punishments, and public praise for individuals should be conveyed sparingly unless the circumstances are most unusual. To praise an individual

Components 9-10: Helping Students to Learn and Grow

publicly for something which does not merit praise, and which the group knows does not deserve praise, is to undermine the significance of praise itself.

(5) *Reporting to the principal.* The absence and tardy reports go to the principal's office; so does a copy of all standardized test results. Copies of the mimeographed report of the month's educational activities and copies of any supplementary curriculum materials would also go to the principal's office. When a child presents a most difficult problem and data are needed on his daily classroom behavior, teachers should keep such records and report them daily. The principal also expects prompt and accurate reports of any accidents that take place or any sudden emergencies which arise. In addition to all this, there are the reports that deal with inventories and requests for teaching materials, equipment, and supplies, including audio-visual aids.

There is still another type of report that is very much needed. We have already remarked that a profession deals with problems, and these problems become publicly known. In the field of medicine, for example, doctors get patients with communicable diseases. In every case these have to be reported to a central source. Year after year, the individual cases are summed; by comparing these yearly reports, informed people can get some idea of the progress or lack of progress in the treatment of these cases.

If one were to read only the official educational reports, one would get the idea that there are no educational problems and no teaching problems. According to the newspapers and magazines, the important problems in the field of education are related to finance, to buildings, grounds, and equipment, to busing, integration, and districting, or to other administrative matters. Much attention currently is being paid to reading and to new projects in math and science.

So far as we know, there is no recording of the number of unusually aggressive children or extremely shy and withdrawn children, or of children in the diagnostic categories relating to thinking and values. There is practically no serious study of morale in classrooms or among teaching staffs.

We believe that if we were to report the numbers of cases in each category and share this knowledge with the community, they would become informed about some of the very serious teaching and learning problems. Names of individual children would not be publicized, but the total number of children in any one school and in the entire district would become known. As one year followed another and with entries being made for each year, all of us would come to know our success or failure in helping children to become more mature and self-directing. We would then be accountable to the public as other professions are. The public would have some idea of whether they were getting what they paid for.

If we were not being successful in some of the areas, we could then pinpoint our difficulties and ask for exactly the kind of consulting service which would be most useful to us. This could draw us into closer association with medical practitioners, sociologists and anthropologists, clinical psychologists, geneticists, and clinical professors of education. Our meetings would then become the first step in an action program—not the mere expenditure of time that characterizes many of our present educational sessions.

This section on reporting would be incomplete without a final suggestion that our reports should also include the ways we have chosen to work with learning problems. If we have valid and reliable records of our failures, we can more easily adapt a change to another alternative instead of continually repeating our past mistakes.

As we make our problems known, the problems which we as teachers actually face, we find new directions for educational research. We might see that a great many alternatives can be tried out under experimental conditions, and the very best ones chosen to guide our work with children.

There is no doubt that *recording and reporting* are indispensable functions of teaching. In cases where they are integrated with our concept of teaching, where we gather data which bears upon the components of teaching, we shall be integrating our efforts for the purposes of improved teaching and taking the community into our confidence. We shall be sharing with them some of the tremendous difficulties involved in guiding the growth and development of children.

WHAT IS TEACHING?

Each of the ten components has been set forth and discussed briefly. An entire volume could have been devoted to each one of them; in the future such expanded attention probably *will* be given to a number of them. The aim here has been to provide enough description and discussion to convey the heart of the matter. In the next and final chapter we have something to say about the list as a totality and about educational administrators, the superintendents and the principals.

THE TEN COMPONENTS OF TEACHING

1. Teaching is informing and explaining.
2. Teaching is showing how.
3. Teaching is supplementing the curriculum.
4. Teaching is providing children with opportunities to think and to share their thoughts with others.
5. Teaching is helping children to develop values.
6. Teaching is relating school and community.
7. Teaching is creating opportunities for each child to earn status and respect among his peers.
8. Teaching is creating a secure emotional atmosphere to facilitate learning.
9. Teaching is diagnosing and remedying learning problems.
10. Teaching is keeping records and reports that are consistent with the other nine functions.

8

For Boards of Education, Superintendents, and Principals

In the cities and towns, in suburbs and rural areas, in public and private schools, in colleges and universities, those people who foot the bills, who pay for the education, do it on *faith alone*. They do not know what they are paying for, and they do not know what they are getting for their money. Among the citizens of our country there is a greater faith in education than there is in religion—a truly amazing, almost unshakeable faith. When the faith is placed in the schools or in the school system, no one sees any need for a critical, searching look at what is going on.

But if our faith is grounded in knowledge about what is going on in the schools, about what the teachers do when they teach, about the concepts, principles, and problems that are discussed, then our faith is an informed faith. Our pride has some basis in reality, and our hopes have some foundation in fact. And, if the facts point to serious shortcomings, we at least know what they are and what we can do about them.

As a general rule, the salaries of administrators and teachers take up from 60 to 85 percent of the school budget. We approve these amounts for the *education* of children. We know that scores on standardized tests do not tell us much about the quality of education in our schools. We also know that the number of high school graduates who go on to college does not tell us much about the quality of education in that high school. Nor does the number of people graduating from our colleges reveal the worth of collegiate education.

What yardstick shall we use? Most boards of education are told that there is no yardstick. Superintendents and principals readily acknowledge that they have few realistic guides to help them when they are observing teachers in action. Teachers believe that principals often make up their minds on the basis of matters that have little to do with teaching itself. Large numbers of teachers have reported that principals seldom visit their classes and superintendents practically never.

Why is this? Both groups of administrators tend to say that they are too busy. Too busy? Too busy to become informed about the ways in which 60 to 85 percent of school money is spent? Are they, in fact, too busy to operate as a principal or as a superintendent? Their jobs call for effective administration of a budget. Are they too busy to see how that money is spent? What is more important than this?

Does the board of education put pressure on the superintendent to make a report each month on the quality of education in the schools? Or do they really want to know? Do they feel some obligation to the community because of the tremendous sums which the community expends for education?

We have heard of teachers who try hard to show at least two hours of films or filmstrips every day to their students. The individual films and filmstrips are said to have little to do with each other. We are told that this procedure makes it possible for the teacher *not to teach*. If he is *not* teaching, should he get a raise every year like those who have dedicated their lives to the education of children?

We know some teachers who actually play detective the major part of each school day. They assign some reading to the class, give them time to read it or require it as homework, and then ask questions to see if the children have indeed read the materials. Assume for a moment that this is being done practically all day long in an elementary school classroom. The community does not need a teacher to perform this function. Anyone could come into the room and find out if the materials had been read. We are all paying for the professional tasks of the teacher. We have a professional obligation to ourselves and to the community to see to it that teachers *teach*.

With the publication of this volume, and assuming that it is widely distributed, we are crossing a divide in American education. A yardstick has been presented to all boards of education, to all superintendents, to all teachers everywhere. The buck cannot be passed anymore. With this volume in their hands board members can say to their superintendent, "We want information from you on the emphasis or lack of it that our teachers give to the thinking processes." This volume has given some very clear guides about this component of teaching. *Any* principal could use these guides and visit every classroom under his general supervision at least two or three times. In every room he could tell immediately whether the teacher is carrying out these processes. He does not have to make guesses about it. After these focused visits, he would be reliably informed about the emphasis which is given to these thinking operations during the period of his visits, and he could make a factual report to his superintendent.

Will the superintendent ask him to do it? Will he insist upon such a report from time to time? Will he accompany the principal on some of the visits? Will these highly paid administrators take education seriously? Will each board of education say: *We are paying for teaching. Are we getting it?* Will it become a board policy to *demand* from the superintendent the data, the hard facts, on this component of teaching? Will boards of education take this responsibility seriously? Will they let the superintendent know that they constitute a board of *education,* not just a finance committee? Will they exert pressure to get information about the quality of the educative experience provided by their schools? Informed citizens of the community will now have a yardstick for measuring the qualities of board members and a yardstick for measuring the quality of the superintendent's annual report.

This volume makes clear *ten* components of teaching. There may be a great many boards of education which may demand the facts with respect to each and every component. Some boards may concern themselves with three or four components just as a starter and insist upon the facts about these. Some boards may start with *just one component,* and they will stick with it until they get the information that they want.

In some communities teachers may be asked to share in the decision on priorities among these ten components. It can be reliably assumed that no teaching group, in any school, will reject *all ten components* as requirements of teaching. Perhaps they will rank them in the order of their importance and then cooperate eagerly with the administration to collect relevant information about those four or five which rank highest. Let it be said again: Until such information is collected, we shall not have a solid basis in fact for answering the question, *What are we paying for, and what are we getting?*

Let us take another component as an example and comment on it, as we have done with the component on thinking processes. In this volume we have said that one of the requirements of teaching is to diagnose learning and behavior difficulties and to make some efforts to remedy them. Let us think for a moment about the national scene. There is great concern about violence. Newspaper articles and editorials emphasize the seriousness of the problem. Books are written about it. TV and radio place a great emphasis upon it. We all wish that it might silently steal away, but we are pretty sure that it won't. In fact, it's becoming a political issue with overtones of racism and poverty.

One of our diagnostic categories describes students who are persistently and characteristically aggressive toward other children and sometimes toward property. These children are often hostile and bellicose; they are often cruel to other children. With habits like this it is often very difficult for them to learn. Where there are untrained teachers, an aggressive child tends to be treated aggressively, but this only aggravates his case further. How many such children are there in each school, and what is the total number in each community? Will these youngsters be among those who someday will be practicing violence in the streets?

Many schools have a number of special services, including school psychologists, social workers, guidance people, and health personnel. All of these people presumably have a background of information and experience to share with others in order to help shape the growth and development of students, especially those students in need of their services.

Could our boards of education ask for semiannual reports concerning, let us say, these extreme cases of aggression? How many such children were reported as of September 1st, at the beginning of a school year? Very specifically, what methods, and materials, and techniques were used to help these children? What were the results? It seems to us that boards of education need this information in order to make policy. They must have the facts; they cannot make educational policy in a vacuum.

The report which goes to them does not need to list the names of the children. The board only needs to know the number of such cases to discover if their educational policies are effective. They cannot make this judgment unless they have facts, probably reported to them by the superintendent of schools, who will insist upon receiving such reports from his principals and his special services departments. But will the boards *demand this information* from their executive?

For Boards of Education, Superintendents, and Principals

From this same component let us take another example. In practically every classroom there is at least one child who seems to be extremely apathetic. He is uninterested in just about every thing that goes on in school. Trying to teach him is like talking to a stone wall. He looks out the window, he fiddles with things in his pockets, he often does not hear questions directed to him—he just doesn't seem to care about anything. And it is very difficult for him to learn. How many of these children are there in any one school, and how many in each school? Perhaps if we had the cold facts, we might find that in one or two schools there are practically none and that in another school there are a great many. How do these schools differ? Perhaps some schools actually create these problems! We probably would not try to find out unless we have information bearing on the question.

Are people who make up the board of education at all interested in what happens to these apathetic children? Are the current operating educational policies effective in working with these children? Or is apathy something like a communicable disease? Where you have a few of these, are you likely to get more? Until we have semiannual reports on these and other kinds of difficulties, we will not know whether our educational policies are effective. We must get the facts. Will the board insist on getting educational reports of this kind from their superintendent? In Chapter 7 of this book, in the section which deals with *diagnosing and remedying*, more than twenty categories of learning problems of major importance are suggested. Many board members, after studying this list, may be very much interested in a selected few of them. They may particularly want reports on at least one from each of the major headings. Data of this kind are absolutely necessary if a board is to discharge its responsibilities intelligently. As we see it, they have only to ask for the information and press for it, and they will get it. Such information can and should be made available to them.

On several occasions we have stated that the *ten components of teaching* have been defined in such a manner that they are easily identifiable when they are being used in the classroom. We have also said that it should not be difficult to report on the activities associated with each component. Perhaps an exception should be made of the very first component, *informing and explaining*, but not very much of an exception. Surely the teacher knows when he is sharing information with children, and he also knows when he is explaining the meanings of some concept, idea, or trend or some scientific or mathematical principle or generalization. How shall all of this be reported? And how can the principal summarize it?

As one possibility, we suggest that each teacher keep a very simple diary-type notebook and that he keep a record that bears upon these questions:

1) Over the designated period of time, what were the significant activities performed by the group? What were the topics to which most attention was given? What did discussion and the sharing of information mainly concern?
2) Within each topic or subject classification, what were the issues, the controversies, and the problems that came up for discussion?
3) With respect to both (1) and (2), what were *the meanings* that received attention? Were they mostly meanings related to what is true or false? Were they meanings dealing with ethical and moral conduct? Were they meanings dealing with the whole aesthetic side of life? Were they intellectual, as in the sense of helping students to understand principles of government? Perhaps they were meanings which helped to answer the question why; in other words, they were the explanations dealing with causes, effects, or correlations.

The principal—alone, or with the cooperation of one or more teachers—would then have the task of summing up these records for one or several grade-groupings. One might say that this is not an altogether simple task, and the pat response to that comment is that ease and simplicity are not criteria for allocating functions to a principal. As was said previously, he is an administrator; he is, as a rule, a high salaried individual with responsibilties for guiding the educational program. Part of his responsibility is to secure valid, reliable evidence about the quality of the educative experience which the students in the schools are having. Most of the entire school budget is spent for this purpose, and it is surely relevant to his functions to pay some attention to the matter.

We have great faith in his abilities to discharge his responsibilities in these matters. Typically, however, the principal does not pay very much intelligent, focused attention to teaching. As he says, he has so many other things to do, many of them of a clerical, routine nature. These not only keep him busy; he seems to *want* to be kept busy by these routine, clerical matters. He steers clear of fundamental questions about education, about teaching, and about reports that might deal with either or both. He seems to like the endless decision making on matters of small import. These functions may be ego-building. They may also be safe in the sense that they divert him and everyone else from his and his staff's primary function: the development of a curriculum that is educative in the senses expressed in this volume, the identification of teaching and non-teaching wherever they make an appearance, and the reporting of all this to the educational authorities of the community.

A FINAL WORD

There are no scapegoats in this volume. We do not hold the principals to blame for the lack of adequate accounting of what goes on in the schools. Yet a systematic approach has to be made. Unless the board of education, the superintendent, the teachers, and the principals work together on this whole matter, there is not much hope—unless we wait for the angry protests of a citizenry that demands the facts, threatens to reject school budgets, and demands a new board if the facts are not forthcoming.

Time is of the essence, and time is running short. As was said earlier, at many levels of education, students and faculty are complaining sharply and frequently about the neglect of *teaching*, and the neglect of quality *education* in our schools. What are the facts? We do not have the facts. But we can get them, and this volume has provided an outline for the identification of *teaching* and for a way of securing evidence that relates to the educational program now in operation.

With this information summarized for them by the principals and by the superintendent of schools, board members will learn something about the educational experiences children are having: they will know what skills are taught, what emphasis is given to thinking, what attention is paid to values, or whether or not the school and the community are enriching each other. In the hands of the board will be information about the creative ways in which teachers are modifying and supplementing the curriculum outline, supplementing texts, and utilizing the new and easily available teaching aids. The board will be informed about the success of the school staff in diagnosing and remedying learning difficulties. It will know a great deal about the morale of the schools, the students, and the faculty. It will know something about the emotional and social climate of all our classrooms, and it will be fully informed about the qualities of the recording and reporting system. This whole array of information, intelligently summarized and presented in a manner that facilitates its comprehension, would help to insure that the board's decisions would be informed decisions, that its vetos would be informed vetos, that its doubts would be informed doubts. It would mean that policy would be supported by fact and interpretation and projection into the near future.

The lay public—the families, the fathers and mothers of our students—would begin to know what education and teaching is all about. People everywhere would know what they are getting for their money, and it is our informed guess that when they know that these ten components of teaching characterize *their* schools, they will have an informed pride and a new faith strengthened by the regular presentation of relevant evidence on educational matters.

References

1. Hill, Clyde M., *et al. Yale-Fairfield Study of Elementary Teaching.* New Haven, Conn.: Yale University Press, 1956.
2. Lasswell, H. D. *Power and Personality.* New York: W. W. Norton & Company, Inc., 1948, pp. 27-29.
3. Lasswell, H. D., and Kaplan, A. *Power and Society.* New Haven, Conn.: Yale University Press, 1950.
4. Openshaw, M. Karl, and Cyphert, Frederick R. *The Development of a Taxonomy for the Classification of Teachers' Classroom Behavior.* Columbus, Ohio: Ohio State University Research Foundation, 1966.
5. Polansky, Lucy. "Group Social Climate and the Teacher's Supportiveness of Group Status Systems," *The Journal of Educational Sociology* (November, 1954), 115-123.
6. Raths, Louis E. "Sociological Knowledge and Needed Curriculum Research," *Research Frontiers in the Study of Children's Learning,* ed. James B. Macdonald. Milwaukee, Wisc.: The University of Wisconsin, School of Education, 1961, pp. 20-48.
7. Raths, Louis E. "The Problem Child." South Orange, N. J.: The Economics Press, 1951.
8. Raths, Louis E., *et al. Teaching for Thinking: Theory and Application.* Columbus, Ohio: Charles E. Merrill Publishing Co., 1967.
9. Raths, Louis E., Harmin, Merrill, and Simon, Sidney B. *Values and Teaching: Working With Values in the Classroom.* Columbus, Ohio: Charles E. Merrill Publishing Co., 1966.

Index

Acceptance, 37-38
Aggression in students, 80
Apathy, 84
Assumptions, 42
Availability of resources, 68

Behavior of teacher, 73
Behavioral limits, 73

Change, 15-16
Classifying, 41
Coding, 42-43
Communication media, 2-3
Comparison, 40
Components of teaching,
    implications of, 25-26
    list of, 24-25
    objections to, 27-31
Cynics, 85
Curriculum supplementation, 24, 38-39
Cyphert, Frederick R., 102

Decision making, 26, 41
Development of a Taxonomy for the Classification of Teachers' Classroom Behavior, The, 15, 102
Dewey, John, 13, 21-22
Diagnosing and remedying learning problems, 24, 31, 77-87
Discipline, 25-26

Education, 1-2
Eliciting values, 49-51
Emotional disturbances, 80

Emotional security, 24, 30-31, 73-75
Evaluation, 42
Extracurricular events, 71

Family and school, 53-55
Family class status, 69
Flightiness of behavior, 84
Functions of teaching,
    formulating list, 18-20
    interpretation of, 20-22

Grade cards, 88
Group power, 62-67

Harmin, Merrill, 102
Health and energy, 68
Health defects, 78-79
Hill, Clyde M., 102
Homogeneous grouping, 29, 38
Hostility in students, 80

Informing and explaining, 24, 34-35, 37
Imagination, 41
Inconsistency of attitudes, 85
Indifference, 84
Individual differences, 71
Inequalities, 65-66
Influence, 68
Interacting with students, 47-49
Interests of students, 71
Interpreting an experience, 41

Kennedy, Robert, 21

Lane, Howard, 38

103

Lasswell, Harold D., 67, 72, 102

Morale, 62-63, 72, 86-87
Motivation of students, 26

National Commission on Teacher Education, 18
New York University, 72
Notebook for teachers, 100

Ohio State University, 15, 18
Openshaw, M. Karl, 102
Overconformity to the teacher, 84
Overdissenters, 84

Parent-Teacher Association, 57-58
Polansky, Lucy, 87, 102
Power, 86-87
Power and Personality, 67
Pretenders, 85
Problem solving, 42
Projects, 42
Psychosomatic disturbances, 81

Raths, Louis E., 102
Reactions of teacher, 46-47
Recording and reporting, 24, 87-92
Rectitude, 68
Regressive behavior, 81
Relating school and community, 24, 28-29, 51-59
Reporting to the principal, 91-92
Reporting to students, 90
Reports to parents,
    oral, 89-90
    written, 88-89
Research, 5-6
Reticence in students, 81
Role players, 85

Schools,
    changes in, 3-4
    as public exhibit, 58-59
Security of students, 73-75
Sense impressions, 40
Showing how, 24, 35-38
Shyness in students, 81
Simon, Sidney B., 102
Skills, 67
Societal problems, 2
Status development, 67-71
Status earning, 24, 29-30, 61-73
Study skills, 80
Submissive behavior, 81
Summarizing, 41

Teacher reaction, 46-47
Teacher's behavior, 73
Teaching,
    components, 23-31
    functions, 16-22
Teaching for Thinking, 40, 83
Thinking, 24, 40-43
Thinking-related behavior, 82-83

Universities,
    admission policies, 7-8
    bureaucracy, 7-10
    failure of, 10-13
University of Wisconsin, 19

Value development, 24, 27-28, 45-51
Value-related behavior, 83-86
Values and Teaching, 45, 47, 84
Values of teacher, 36-38
Violence in students, 80

Withdrawing in students, 81
Work habits, 80

Yale-Fairfield Study of Elementary Teaching, The, 15